The Art of Facilitation

How to Create Group Synergy

Dale Hunter □ Anne Bailey □ Bill Taylor

FISHER
er
BOOKS™

Library of Congress Cataloging-in-Publication Data

Hunter, Dale, 1943-
  The art of facilitation: how to
  create group synergy/Dale Hunter,
  Anne Bailey, Bill Taylor.
    p. cm.
  Includes bibliographical references
  and index.
  ISBN 1-55561-101-X(pb)
  1.   Communication in small groups.
  2.   Decision-making, Group. 3. Small
      groups. 4. Social facilitaition. I. Bailey,
  Anne, 1944-. II. Taylor, Bill, 1942-.
  III. Title.
  HM133.H86 1995
302.3'4—dc20   95-31909
                 CIP

Originally published in 1992
By Tandem Press, Auckland

10 MV 03 02

Fisher Books is a member of the Perseus Books Group.

Find us on the World Wide Web at http://www.fisherbooks.com

Fisher Books are available at special discounts for bulk purchases in the U.S. by corporations, institutions, and other organizations. For more information, please contact the Special Markets Department at the Perseus Books Group, 11 Cambridge Center, Cambridge, MA 02142, or call (617) 252-5298.

Notice: The information in this book is true and complete to the best of our knowledge. It is offered with no guarantees on the part of the authors or Fisher Books. The authors and publisher disclaim all liability in connection with use of this book.

Welcome

Welcome to everyone working in groups.
Welcome to the art of facilitation.

We invoke the spirit of cooperation through the ages—past,
present and future—and welcome into existence the word
"cooperacy," a new distinction which brings forth government
through cooperation.

We acknowledge our families, communities, networks and all the
groups which have *grown* us.

Ask me what is the most important thing in the world
and I will tell you
it is people, it is people, it is people.

The Taste of Banzo's Sword

Matajuro Yagyu was the son of a famous swordsman. His father, believing that his son's work was too mediocre to anticipate mastership, disowned him.

So Matajuro went to Mt. Futara to find Banzo, the famous swordsman. But Banzo confirmed the father's judgment. "You wish to learn swordsmanship under my guidance?" asked Banzo. "You cannot fulfill the requirements."

"But if I work hard, how many years will it take me to become a master?" persisted the youth.

"The rest of your life," replied Banzo.

"I cannot wait that long," explained Matajuro. "I am willing to pass through any hardship if only you will teach me. If I become your devoted servant, how long might it be?"

"Oh, maybe 10 years," Banzo relented.

"My father is getting old and soon I must take care of him," continued Matajuro. "If I work far more intensively, how long would it take me?"

"Oh, maybe 30 years," said Banzo.

"Why is that?" asked Matajuro. "First you say 10 and now 30 years. I will undergo any hardship to master this art in the shortest time!"

"Well," said Banzo, "in that case you will have to remain with me for 70 years. A man in such a hurry as you are to get results seldom learns quickly."

"Very well," declared the youth, understanding at last that he was being rebuked for impatience. "I agree."

Matajuro was told never to speak of fencing and never to touch a sword. He cooked for his master, washed the dishes, made his bed, cleaned the yard, cared for the garden—all without a word of swordsmanship.

Three years passed. Still Matajuro labored on. Thinking of his future, he was sad. He had not even begun to learn the art to which he had devoted his life.

But one day Banzo crept up behind him and gave him a terrific blow with a wooden sword.

The following day, when Matajuro was cooking rice, Banzo again sprang upon him unexpectedly.

After that, day and night, Matajuro had to defend himself from unexpected thrusts. Not a moment passed in any day that he did not have to think of the taste of Banzo's sword.

Matajuro learned so rapidly that he brought smiles to the face of his master. He became the greatest swordsman in the land.

Contents

Introduction

The Earth is running out of energy resources, but there is a
source of special energy which has scarcely been tapped. It is
the power available in groups, the power of group synergy.
Tapping into group synergy is made possible through powerful
group facilitation.

Effective group facilitation is an artful dance requiring rigorous
discipline. The role of the facilitator offers an opportunity to
dance with life on the edge of a sword, to be present and aware,
to be with and for people in a way that cuts through to what
enhances and fulfills life. A facilitator is a peaceful warrior.

Group facilitation is moment-by-moment awareness; it is being
awake and being in action—awake in the way a hunter stalks a
tiger or a mother watches over her newborn infant. The facilitator
protects the group culture, at the same time cutting through
unproductive or sabotaging patterns to get to what enhances and
fulfills the group purpose.

This book reveals the secrets of the art of facilitation. It provides
access to the source of group empowerment and shows how to
create this with ease.

The Art of Facilitation is the second book by the authors of *The
Zen of Groups—A Handbook for People Meeting with a Purpose*. That
book focuses on the role of the group member and explores how
effectiveness can be vastly increased through accessing synergy.
The Art of Facilitation provides a deeper cut into developing group
effectiveness by focusing on the role and skills of the facilitator.

The purpose of the book is also to provide a training resource for facilitators, and to enable group members to understand and take on this role.

The book is in four parts. Part 1 draws on the cooperative beliefs and values underlying facilitation and examines in depth the art of intervention, which is the working mode of the facilitator. Part 2 is a toolkit of facilitative designs and processes, including a facilitation training program. Part 3 provides a personal perspective on facilitation through four interviews—one with each of the three authors, the fourth with John Heron, a leading facilitator with whom all the authors have studied. Part 4 provides some additional resources.

When working with groups, the authors use the first person *we* to include themselves in any statements. In this book, we have mainly used the second person *you* to address the reader directly. This does not imply we know better or that we are separating ourselves from the reader. On the contrary, we find it empowering to know that we don't know and that we are always learning and in training.

The authors wish to thank Tony Coates and the members of the First Advanced Facilitation Training Group held at the Kohia Teachers' Center in 1993. Scattered throughout this book are some wonderful insights into the art of facilitation, courtesy of the members of that training group and the editors at Fisher Books. Look for these gems in boxes.

Part 1
Facilitation

Preparing the Ground

What is Facilitation?

Facilitation is about process—*how you do something*—rather than the content—*what you do*. A facilitator is a *process guide*, someone who makes a process easier or more convenient. Facilitation is about *movement*—moving something from A to B. The facilitator guides the group toward a *destination*. Facilitation makes it easier to get to an agreed destination.

Facilitate = to make easy or more convenient.

You can facilitate yourself, another person or a group. This book is primarily about facilitating groups. However, to facilitate groups effectively you need to facilitate yourself—your own processes (external and internal). And you need to be able to facilitate others individually as well (coaching or one-to-one facilitation), because groups are made up of individual people who come together to fulfill a particular purpose.

So, to become a powerful and effective group facilitator you need to train yourself in self-facilitation, the facilitation of others and the facilitation of a group.

What are the beliefs behind facilitation?

Why are we focusing on facilitation rather than other ways of working with groups, such as management, team leadership or being a boss?

The main belief behind group facilitation is that full cooperation between all people is both possible and desirable—values of equality, shared decision-making, equal opportunity, power sharing and personal responsibility are basic to full cooperation.

The skills of group facilitation grew out of cooperative movements around the world and are based on ensuring that everyone in a group can, if they wish, fully participate in all decisions that affect them.

Our society has a democratic model—not a cooperative one. Democracy requires cooperation between people and participation in decision-making, but says that the majority is right and majority decision-making is the best way to make decisions.

If you draw a continuum of decision-making, with autocracy (one person deciding on behalf of all the rest) at one end, you will see that cooperacy (new word) is at the other end, with democracy in between.

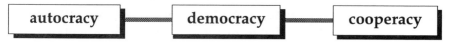

autocracy — democracy — cooperacy

We are not saying democracy or autocracy are wrong. Both are useful and have a place in decision-making. However, we have a bias towards cooperacy and believe it is not used more often because its skills are not part of our culture. People want full cooperation and participation, but when it comes to the crunch, they believe the only thing to do is to take a vote and have the majority rule.

The shift from democracy to cooperacy is of the same magnitude as the historical shift from feudalism (autocracy) to democracy, and will be as big a culture shift. It could also be described in personal development terms as the shift from dependence (autocracy) through independence (democracy) to interdependence (cooperacy).

Most people know something of committee procedure and rules, and how to take a majority vote—these skills are very much part of our culture. However, when you want to reach a consensus or collective decision, you can often become frustrated as it seems too hard to get everyone to agree. You believe it is impossible or impractical:

It would take too long to get agreement.

We'd still be here next week.

Our business would go under while we fooled around.

These comments are often the immediate reaction to the idea of using cooperative decision-making.

The authors have learned many of the skills needed to make cooperative decision-making a practical and workable alternative to democratic or autocratic models. We want to pass these skills on to everyone so people can have a real choice as to what model they use. We want cooperative processes to be as well known and accessible as committees and majority voting.

We believe using cooperative methods makes it possible to access more easily a very important and critical resource for the world. That resource is *group synergy*—the alternative fuel for the twenty-first century.

We may be running out of some key energy resources, but group synergy is one which has scarcely been tapped. We are in kindergarten in relation to working together as groups, organizations, businesses and nations. The planet needs group synergy to survive because it is group effort on both a small and a large scale which will save and heal our planet.

So you can see we are very serious about writing this book. Our mission is to contribute to creating synergy on the planet.

It is important to mention here that we assume group synergy is a neutral resource like oil or coal—that it can be used for good or ill. So we need to do our very best to pass these skills on with care and integrity. However, we believe group synergy at a higher level is not ultimately neutral—that on a global scale it will only be positive.

Over the last 30 years a lot of work has been done in personal development. It has now spread throughout much of the world and individuals have undertaken a wide range of personal development methods. Much of this work has been done in groups although the focus has been mainly on individual growth and development.

We believe there is now a quantum leap ready to happen—that of *group consciousness*. Foreshadowed by family therapy, organizational development research and experience gained by living in communities, we are now in the pioneering stage of this quantum shift in human consciousness. We believe it will open up possibilities we can barely dream about. For the planet to survive, this leap is imperative.

The role of the facilitator

The role of the facilitator is somewhat similar to that of the chairperson of a majority-voting model such as a committee.

The facilitator knows how to guide a group of people through cooperative processes, including collective decision-making, so that the group can fulfill its purpose as easily as possible.

Before we wrote this book, we wrote *The Zen of Groups—A Handbook for People Meeting with a Purpose*. That book provides the concepts and tools to be an effective member of a cooperative group. If you are new to this kind of group, we suggest you read that book first. This book is a resource for people to facilitate cooperative groups. It contains the concepts and tools for working effectively and powerfully with cooperative groups.

Key concepts

For the purpose of clarity and completeness, the key concepts from *The Zen of Groups* are briefly outlined here:

Individual uniqueness—Each member of the group is unique and has his or her own world view expressed through ideas, beliefs, culture, memories and behavior patterns.

Baggage—This is everything you bring to the group—ideas, beliefs, opinions, feelings, desires, patterns, hopes and fears (your identity). It is all those things which can get in the way of your being fully present, moment by moment, to yourself and others.

Leadership—This comes out of the group. A leader can lead only with the active or tacit agreement of the group. There are no leaders without groups, though there can be groups without leaders.

Power—Power is always a factor in group life, and power issues need to be identified and worked through. There are different kinds of power—positional power, assigned power, knowledge power, personal power and factional power. Aim to share power as much as possible.

Feelings—Feelings are important and need to be acknowledged. They are not rational. Group members need to learn to have feelings, rather than be had by them.

Trust and identity—A group develops trust and identity through sharing. Attending to leadership, power issues and feelings will encourage the bonding of group members, leading to a stronger group identity and deepening trust.

Stages in the life of a group—Groups have a life cycle and move through various stages before reaching maturity. Most groups never reach maturity but get stuck, and do not have the skills to work through conflicts and power issues and readily access synergy.

Roles people play—There are lots of behavioral roles you play in groups; some are constructive, some not. Avoid getting stuck in a particular role—for example, placater, blocker, tension-reliever, devil's advocate.

Process and task—*Group process* is about taking care of the group members as they fulfill their task—that is, the project, objective or purpose of the group.

Group-assigned roles—A group will assign the roles of facilitator, recorder and timekeeper. Roles can be rotated to increase participation and skill learning. A facilitator can also be brought in from outside the group if more objectivity is needed. The facilitator does not take part in the content of decisions and cannot vote.

Group purpose—Every group needs to be clear about its purpose. A group without a purpose is purposeless, and therefore ineffective.

Ground rules—These can be set by the group to clarify and protect how it will operate. They may address confidentiality, being on time, personal responsibilities or any matters of concern to the group. Ground rules need to matter or it is better not to set them.

Being present—You are partly *unconscious* most of the time and so not fully present to yourself and others. *Being present* is an ongoing, moment-by-moment discipline. In addition, you get tripped up by your baggage (see above) and are not *all there*.

Speaking and listening—Being in a group is about speaking and listening, but especially listening. The more skills you have in communication, the better.

Withholding—Withholding is not saying things which need to be said to have you fully present in the group. You withhold out of fear. If you keep thinking about something and not being present in the group, there is something you are withholding. Sharing "withholds" can be scary at first, but it deepens the trust in the group and takes it into the synergy zone.

Conflict—Conflict is normal in groups. It needs to be attended to and worked through promptly. Unattended conflicts become skeletons in the closet that come back to haunt the group. (See Chapters 7 and 8 for more on conflict.)

Collective (or consensus) decision-making—This means that everyone agrees on every decision. (See Chapter 7.)

2 Facilitating Yourself

Facilitating yourself is about going on a journey for life—a scary and exciting journey which will take you to places within yourself which will surprise, delight and disgust you. Facilitating yourself is about *self-awareness*.

The way we grow and develop ourselves as conscious human beings is by facilitating ourselves and being facilitated by others. This happens on emotional, mental and spiritual levels.

Much of our physical development is also self-facilitated. Your body shape, tone and stamina are affected by exercise. You can modify your body to build up certain muscle groups to perform special functions as sportspeople, musicians, dancers and singers do.

Many people in the healing professions now believe that sickness, including life-threatening illnesses such as cancer and AIDS, and healing of the body are largely influenced by the mind (our thoughts). There is a universal acceptance of the importance of healthy food on the development and maintenance of the body, although there is incessant debate on what is the *right* food. Clean air and absence of toxic substances from the body are also recognized as important to healthy living and the length of our lives.

You could debate to what extent physical, emotional, mental and spiritual development is natural (just happens), or is facilitated by yourself or others. But the debate is not important. Why not consider that most of your development is self-facilitated and that you can increase this through your own actions? That way you take responsibility for your own development.

Being with yourself

The first step in facilitating yourself is to *be with yourself.* To get access to being with yourself, it will help to consider the following questions:

Are you comfortable with yourself the way you are right now?

Are you comfortable with your body?

Are you comfortable with your feelings?

Are you comfortable with your thoughts?

Are you comfortable with your sex and sexual orientation?

Are you comfortable with your cultural and national affinities?

Are you okay about being you?

Many people live lives of quiet desperation.

I'm not okay, and I hope you don't find out how awful I am.

Life is a process of covering up and compensating for your own *not-okayness.*

Before you get involved in facilitating other people, you need to accept yourself and continue to work on this. Facilitating yourself is about growing, developing and training yourself—but not about fixing yourself. Do you get a sense of the difference? Fixing is always about compensating for something being wrong—it actually holds *wrong* in place.

Accepting ourselves is the biggest hurdle for most people:

I accept myself completely.

I am a magnificent human being

I am fully alive now

Empowering yourself

Through self-facilitation you can empower yourself. Empowerment is *coming into your own unique place of power where you are most truly your own self.* It is about recognizing when you are in *your power* and how you experience this, and bringing it into all aspects of your life. It is about being at home in your body and in your personal space. It does not always mean being strong and confident—you may be most *in your power* when you are feeling very vulnerable. It is more to do with being truly authentic and present.

Being strong and confident over the top of nervousness and vulnerability will be experienced by others as a cover-up or perhaps a sense of incongruence they can't put their finger on. When you are in your power, your words and actions have a different ring to them—things happen more spontaneously and you have access to synchronicity and miracles. You can train yourself to keep coming back *into your power* and get others to coach you when they notice you are out of your *place of power*.

> **When you are in your power, your words and actions have a different ring to them**

Passive and proactive

Self-facilitation is about empowering yourself. You can do this *passively* or *proactively*. Passive self-facilitation happens when you put yourself into a situation where things will happen to you which you believe will be empowering. You may choose to live in a particular house with ready-made roommates or to work at a particular workplace with other people. You may enroll in some kind of training program. You may choose to watch a movie or go to certain restaurants or bars or vacation in a particular place.

By placing yourself in certain situations, you are provided with experiences which affect you more or less profoundly. An extreme example would be if you sat in the middle of a busy road at night—you would be passively facilitating getting yourself killed or injured. This is unlikely to be empowering.

Proactive self-facilitation occurs when you consciously choose to alter your behavior—to interrupt how you normally do things, believing this can benefit you. You may choose to speak or listen or behave in a new way. Or, begin meditating, expressing feelings you usually hide, sharing secrets, wearing different clothes, and so on. You take the initiative—it is your idea, your choice, your action.

You can allow and move through the thoughts, feelings and body sensations which resist the change in behavior, and use your will as the impetus or touchstone to keep you on course. Exercise your free will. As you become more and more proactive, your will also becomes stronger. Just as starting a fitness program will develop and strengthen your body, exercising your will to change your behavior develops and strengthens the will—and your capacity to be proactive.

Self-facilitation as a training tool

For a facilitator-in-training, self-facilitation is essential. You need to take on training yourself to be fully conscious and awake as much as possible. How can you usefully facilitate others if you don't facilitate yourself? This would be hypocritical. As a facilitator, you need to be constantly in training and working on yourself. You need to be an Olympic athlete in self-awareness. Ask yourself:

> *To what extent am I responsible for my own actions?*
>
> > > *my own thoughts?*
> > >
> > > *my own emotions?*
> > >
> > > *my own physical sensations?*
> > >
> > > *my own environment?*
> > >
> > > *my own relationships with others?*

> *Right now can I choose my own thoughts?*
>
> > *my own feelings?*
> >
> > *my own physical sensations?*
> >
> > *my own actions?*
> >
> > *my physical environment?*

> *What about now?*
>
> *And now?*
>
> *Perhaps now then?*
>
> *Or now?*

Start to observe yourself and keep observing yourself as often as you can remember. Write the following question on a card and place it on your desk or mirror.

What am I choosing now?

Am I choosing to be well?

to be loved?

to be comfortable?

to be stimulated?

to be bored?

to be sad?

to suffer?

Doing this exercise is very useful as it will assist you to become more self-aware. And there is no right answer. The value is in the looking.

What fascinating choices you have every moment!

Perhaps each moment you have a choice to

expand—give—contribute—appreciate—live

or to

contract—take—pull back—criticize—die

The usefulness of this inquiry process is that you look at yourself and develop some awareness other than your thoughts, feelings and body sensations.

Consider the possibility that you are totally responsible for all your thoughts, feelings, body sensations, physical environment, people you are with, and all your circumstances (food, money, clothing, housing, belongings). You don't have to believe it is completely true, although it may well be, but just consider the possibility to see what alters when you take on this way of being in the world.

Try it as an exercise. As you experiment with this for a while (days, weeks) ask yourself the following questions:

What do I choose to learn from this (choice, situation)?

If I am choosing to be sad, angry, upset, ill, what can I learn from this?

How is this fulfilling my present needs?

How is this situation fulfilling my beliefs about myself, about others, about the world?

This inquiry process is only for use on yourself. Don't apply it to others. It is about developing your awareness, not assessing others—that would entirely miss the point.

One way to be with others is to notice that:

They are choosing to do . . .

to say . . .

to be . . .

How interesting! This is where they are choosing to be. It may be life-enhancing or not for them. Only they will know.

To be a facilitator requires you to extend and develop the part of yourself which can give *free attention*—that part of your awareness not caught up with thoughts, feelings and body sensations. To do this you need to explore and find personal development methods that will enable you to heal old upsets (from the past). Upsets are *set-ups for you to grow*. They are often from your early childhood, when you were very impressionable.

There is a wide range of personal development methods to choose from, including action methods, co-counseling, primal therapy, rebirthing, voice dialogue, psychodrama, encounters, neurolinguistic programming, and so on.

Other methods to increase your available free attention are also useful. These include meditation, prayer, creative visualization and ritual groups.

Upset

You also need to develop ongoing practices to help you avoid picking up more upsets (baggage) than you already have. You need clearing and protecting techniques to do this. See Process 11 of the Toolkit, page 156.

If you are upset for more than, say, two minutes, something has been activated from the past—the upset is no longer solely in the present. It helps to look at what has been triggered from the past—what specific incidents spring to mind and how you can heal or complete these.

One of the authors, Dale Hunter, says:

There are several ways I handle my own old upsets when they get triggered. One way is to acknowledge the upset (I may be feeling angry or scared or sad and am not sure what it's about) and keep doing what I have to do to keep my commitments. I put the upset on hold. If the upset is related to a particular person I know well, I will request a clearing session with them. [See Process 11a of the Toolkit, page 158.]

I may also work with another facilitator, using co-counseling or other techniques to access the cause of the upset and begin the healing process. Another process I use to release and transform the energy of an upset is vigorous dancing or going to the gym.

What I often do is take time out and fully explore the feelings that have come up. I call this my healing process. I like to do this by myself. I lie down on the sofa under my favorite blanket, relax and begin to breathe into the feelings, allowing them to totally reveal themselves, in their fullness, so that nothing is left unfelt. I relax into them, no matter how awful they seem at the time. I give up any resistance to them—any judgment of them. This is a very healing process for me. I stay with and allow the feelings for as long as it takes—it could be half an hour to several hours.

Usually I will slip into a meditative space and become very sensitive to my body energy, and sounds and movement around me. I keep watching my breathing and relaxing my body. After a time (and this varies enormously) there will be a shift in my consciousness. The feelings will begin to move and dissipate as though they have had their say and been listened to. Often during this process, I have insights and visual or word images that clarify the nature and source of the upset and suggest ways I might do some things differently. After this process I am freed up, clearer and less at the mercy of those particular feelings. They have loosened their grip.

Upsets are a bit like children, demanding to be heard and given full attention. When they are fully heard, they become satisfied and contented. This is my favorite way of facilitating my own emotional healing.

We suggest you experiment and explore a range of techniques and processes to find the ones that work best for you. There is no right answer here. It is a personal matter. Be gentle and tender with yourself—a loving parent. (Usually you are far more critical of yourself than anyone else is ever likely to be.) As you try things out and get to know yourself, your confidence in your own choices and your own truth will grow. Trust yourself and your wisdom. Self-facilitation is the key to the effective facilitation of others.

Although it is easier to see other people's blocks, seeing and healing your own is a vital, ongoing and lifetime journey with many joys and challenges along the way. It is a process. There are times when the way is clear. At other times nothing is clear. The process is like going down a tunnel, seeing a dim light at the end, moving through the tunnel and coming out into the light— then going into another tunnel and repeating the process over and over.

> **Knowing others is wisdom.**
> **Knowing the self is enlightenment.**
> (Lao Tsu)

Facilitating Others

One-to-one facilitation

Like facilitating yourself, facilitating *another person*—one-to-one facilitation—is important in training for facilitating groups. This chapter is an introduction only, but covers the essentials you need to be aware of in facilitating another person. It is not intended to be comprehensive—there is plenty of written material and training available for one-to-one work.

It is important to distinguish between therapeutic facilitation and facilitation of healthy people. We are writing here about *healthy people*—not those requiring therapy. If you are facilitating someone and you feel out of your depth, or if he or she is very fearful, acts strangely or doesn't seem to be getting anything out of the conversation, don't persevere. Contact a more-experienced facilitator or therapist for your own coaching or recommend that the person see a doctor or therapist.

Facilitation is not giving advice

Facilitating another person tends to come more easily than facilitating yourself. You see other people's patterns and blocks more easily than your own. Often you want to tell others what to do. This is called *giving advice*.

Advice is telling someone what you think he or she ought to do. It comes from "I know better." Advice is not facilitative, especially if it is not requested. Even if it is requested, it is often not helpful because it fails to take into account that everyone is different and unique and will choose different experiences and learning.

Facilitation recognizes that each person is perfect just the way he or she is—each person is already whole and complete (and this includes having problems and difficulties like all other human beings). The values of respect, honor, accomplishment, fulfillment and integrity underlie facilitation.

I respect and honor you. It is a privilege for me to be with you and you with me. We matter. Our time together matters.

This attitude of respect and honor is necessary before you can facilitate someone. By *attitude,* we mean where you as facilitator are coming from or where you are *standing.* You will come from not assessing or judging people or taking account of society's view of them. You will accept them as whole people with their own values, behaviors and world view.

If your attitude is that there is something wrong with the person you are to facilitate, then you will think he or she needs to be fixed—with or without your help. This is more of *I know better*

Facilitation calls forth people's best intentions.

and implies you know what the person *being fixed* looks like. This is not a powerful place for a facilitator to come from.

Another way of saying this is that you need to accept people the way they are if you are going to work with them as their facilitator. This does not mean you need to like them or agree with them. But if you are unable to honor, respect and be with them, you cannot facilitate them.

If you are asked to give advice ("What do you think I should do?") to another person or in a group, you might use one of the following responses. All redirect the question to the advice seeker.

> *I notice a "should" in there. Have you got some judgments or assessments about what is the right thing to do?*
>
> *What alternatives can you generate for yourself?*
>
> *I suggest you answer that question for yourself.*
>
> *Would you like the group to generate some suggestions?*
>
> *Are you asking for my opinion?*
>
> *Is it illegal, immoral or unhealthy?*
>
> *If illegal: What is the law?*
>
> *If immoral: What is the principle or belief?*
>
> *If unhealthy: What is the risk?*

Being with another

Facilitating another person requires being able to be with him or her. First, it involves being with yourself, in your own body, your own space, with your own thoughts and feelings, and being comfortable and at home with who you are. Second, it involves being with another, being comfortable and at home with him or her. Ask yourself the following questions:

Am I comfortable being with (name)?

Am I comfortable with his or her body?

Am I comfortable with his or her appearance?

Am I comfortable with his or her voice?

Am I comfortable with his or her expression of feelings?

Am I comfortable with his or her expression of thoughts?

Am I comfortable with his or her sex or sexual orientation?

Am I comfortable with his or her ethnic group or culture?

Is he or she okay?

If you can be with another person with respect and honor—not wanting to make him or her different or better—you are ready to learn about facilitating others. Also see Being with Another, Process B1 of the Toolkit, page 141.

Living in different worlds

Everyone has a view of the world. Every view of the world is different. Everyone lives in different worlds.

I have a view of the world.

My world view is unique.

This world view is all-encompassing.

This is the way the world is.

You have a world view.

Your world view is unique.

Your world view is all-encompassing.

This is the way the world is.

It is easy to assume that someone else's world is the same as or similar to your own. Your way of experiencing the world is the way the world is. You assume others perceive (see/feel/think) things in the same way that you do. Otherwise how can you understand them?

Consider the possibility that you can never fully understand other people. Their mix of life experience (including culture, sex, communities of interest and place, family, schooling, friends, age, work, recreation, values and beliefs) will always differ from your own. They are always a mystery. This is both the joy and frustration of being with other people. You can have moments of being *at one*, but this will not be ongoing.

What often happens is that people make a mental jump from seeing that another's perceptions are different to assuming that their own perceptions are better.

The way I see things is right. The way you see them is wrong.

or

My experience with (childhood, school, marriage, work) was . . . ;
   therefore you must have had similar experiences.

or

I believe . . . about (sex, religion, marriage, politics, and so on).
   Surely you must have similar beliefs.

or

I feel strongly about (abortion, the environment, child abuse, the role
   of women, and so on). Surely you must feel strongly about these
   things too.

If another person's behavior, beliefs and values are unacceptable to you (and some people's will be), say so and don't work with him or her as a facilitator. It is important to recognize your own limits and not to pretend to be more accepting than you really are. You may be able to refer the person to someone who has more experience or a world-view that is more similar. Also see My World, Your World, Process B3 of the Toolkit, page 144.

Projection

Another thing to get more conscious about is how you project your world (your past experiences) onto other people and situations. You do this all the time. This is the way you make sense of and interpret the world. It can be a safety mechanism to help you recognize danger quickly. It also acts as a filter to experiencing the present directly.

Consider that you are blinded by your projections. You mostly see things through a *projection fog*, playing your old movie over the top of what is happening now and connecting the moment-by-moment present with your past. You may often disappointed in or surprised by other people because they do not fit your preconceived picture of how they might behave—based on other people you have known in the past who resemble them in some way. So you are often relating to a projected person rather than the real one who is with you.

You also live out your unresolved past experiences through new scenarios:

> *All tall dark men remind me of my father and my unresolved feelings about him. I never date anyone who looks like that as all my unresolved feelings are stirred up immediately. I avoid those guys like the plague.*

*When anyone looking like or behaving like my mother is my boss,
the relationship is difficult. I always end up feeling misunder-
stood and unappreciated. It is so stupid. Even though I now have
some consciousness about this, I still seem to have this automatic
reaction.*

Such is the power of projections.

The identity check exercises (Processes B7 and B8 of the
Toolkit, pages 151-152) are very useful for identifying your own
projections about people and situations. The first time one of the
authors, Dale Hunter, did this exercise was at a co-counseling
training course in 1979.

*We did the identity check in pairs and then shared in the whole
group. There were 30 people there and we were sitting in a large
circle. I have never forgotten the shock of looking around the room
and "seeing" my mother, sisters, childhood friends, and adults I
had known as a child, all present in the circle. I had been
projecting my early world onto the present and was relating to all
these people as though they were my family, early friends and
associates. The people I warmed to reminded me of people I liked
from the past and the people I was not attracted to reminded me of
people who were associated with unpleasant memories.*

You are usually unaware of the power of projections and have
no idea that most of your experience of the world is perceived
secondhand through your version of reality.

Listening

Communication has been described as 80 percent listening and
20 percent speaking. Listening is a very important part of facilitation. Listening powerfully is a skill and a way of being with
people. Listening can be full of assessments and judgments about

the person being listened to, or it can be a period of time-out from speaking yourself when you mentally rehearse your own lines or fantasize about other things triggered by the conversation.

Alternatively, listening can be a powerful energy which draws forth the speaking of the other person and honors the magnificence of the speaker. The listener can listen actively for the *gold* in the speaking, and create such a positive listening energy that the speaker will begin to speak and share himself or herself in a totally new way. Perhaps you can recall someone listening to you like this—you felt 10 feet tall, powerful and honored.

As a facilitator you need to be training your listening constantly. Listen to each person you come in contact with as though he or she is the most important person in the world. The irony is that the conversation you are having is indeed the most important one at that moment. Listen as though your life depends on it. Listen for the commitments, the dreams, the love, the vulnerability of the speaker. Listen for what lights the speaker up and gives enjoyment to his or her life. Listen in the speaking for what expands, energizes and enlivens.

As your listening develops, you will be amazed how magnificent every person is and how love is present in all of your conversations.

Listen also for the conversation itself. What is being said and what is not being said? What is spoken from the heart ("I feel") as opposed to from the head ("I think")? Is the speaking a series of complaints, blaming others, self-criticism and descriptions of events, or is it creating a vision or dream, and opportunities to have this happen through action? What happens at the beginning, middle and end of the conversation (the structure)? Is the conversation left hanging in the air or is it complete and with opportunities for action?

Speaking—interventions

Out of powerful listening comes *facilitative speaking*. This is speaking which empowers the listener. Facilitation involves the use of questions and suggestions (*interventions*) to encourage the other person to clarify and explore his or her own thoughts and feelings. The person can then move forward in line with the insights and connections he or she makes. Facilitating a person is about empowering him or her to:

Fulfill his or her dreams.

Create something new.

Have something happen that will make a difference in his or her own life and in their world.

Catch his or her own patterns and blocks.

Identify what he or she wants to happen next.

Facilitation is not about interpreting someone else's world. Interpretations are only valid or useful if there is agreement by the other person. And it is not about giving advice or your opinion.

Facilitative speaking can be reflective.

You can reflect back the content of what has been said:

What you have said is . . .

What I heard you say is . . .

Or you can reflect back the spirit of what has been said in an empowering way:

I can hear that you are concerned about . . .

are committed to . . .

are making a contribution towards . . . project through . . .

have a vision about . . .

want to do something about . . .

are accomplished at . . .

See Mining the Gold, Process B4 of the Toolkit, page 146.

Interrupting disempowering conversations

Our first response to upset is usually to blame or discount ourselves or others. Facilitative speaking will interrupt the conversations that disempower the speaker.

> *I notice you said you are hopeless at that. Can you say that some other way that is more empowering? (For example, "This is an area I am training in.")*

> *I notice you said you should do that—it sounds as if you don't have a choice. Is that so?*

> *I notice you said you can never remember names. Could you say that in a way that doesn't reinforce your forgetfulness? (For example, "In the past I have found it difficult to remember names, but I am now remembering names more and more easily.")*

See Empowering Interpretations, Process B6, page 150.

Facilitative speaking will also interrupt conversations in which the speaker disempowers others by blaming. The facilitator is not there as a *blame policeperson*, but rather as someone who notices the blaming and encourages the other person to move through and see it as a preliminary to understanding the underlying issue. Blaming is often the way we find out how we feel about something, so the facilitator will encourage the client to explore this— maybe by exaggerating the blaming until it becomes ridiculous.

Blame. . . blame. . . blame. . . blame. . . oops!

What is my role or responsibility in this?

Remember, blaming is always disempowering, at least for the speaker, and is always about avoiding responsibility. Caution: People are so attached to blaming that this may not be a popular idea.

Encouraging lightness

Humor is another way to interrupt disempowering conversations—if you can see the lighter side to a problem, your perception of it often shifts. Gently encourage the person to see the humor in the situation. If handled sensitively, the person will be able to laugh gently at himself or herself.

I suppose my shouting at the boss, stomping out and tripping as I left was quite reminiscent of Charlie Chaplin. I missed the opportunity to throw a pie at him, though.

Coaching

An important part of one-to-one facilitation is *coaching.* Coaching can be directive and includes confronting another person when requested. The facilitator coaches only when asked. I may request coaching from you. You may request coaching from me.

Sometimes it is also appropriate to offer coaching. "Would you like some coaching on that?" A request or an offer can be accepted or declined freely and this needs to be made very clear. To decline coaching does not mean anything about you or the other person; it is merely an ongoing choice.

To train yourself to coach others one-to-one, it is important to have lots of experience in being coached yourself.

Coaching is a contractual arrangement. Without agreement it is potentially abusive. So let's say someone has requested coaching or a facilitated session with you, you understand he or she is well, and you have agreed to facilitate him or her. You now have a contract.

Coaching for action

If the person you are coaching has decided to take some action, he or she may request support by way of ongoing coaching. This will take the form of encouraging the person to invent and carry out the actions necessary to accomplish the plans and projects. Coaching is particularly helpful when the going gets tough and lots of reasons come up (disempowering conversations) as to why, in retrospect, a project may not be such a great idea.

Some coaching interventions are:

What is something you can do to have . . . happen?

What resources do you have or need to do that?

Is there anything stopping you from having that happen?

Is there a small step you can take now toward that larger project?

Can you draw up a plan which will get you from A to B?

What support will you need to implement your plan?

For example, the friend who yelled at the boss may have decided another appointment is needed to clean up the issue, but may need encouragement to make the appointment.

Perhaps this person has a pattern of stewing over incidents like this for days or weeks rather than going back and cleaning it up quickly. It is something he or she wants to do, but procrastinates because it seems scary.

You can offer such encouragements as:

When will you make the appointment?

I request that you phone me at 5 p.m. and confirm that you have made the appointment.

What is it that you want to say to him? Will that be complete for you then?

How can you ensure that you do say that? Do you need to write it down?

Phone me after the meeting, say by 3 p.m.

This kind of ongoing coaching is becoming popular in business. It is all about interrupting your patterns, particularly those which get in the way of (sabotage) your doing what you really want to do.

Training

We suggest you develop your listening and speaking skills through participation in experiential training programs such as co-counseling, neurolinguistic programming, voice dialogue or psychodrama. Training programs in counseling skills may also be useful.

These experiential training programs will also train you in one-to-one facilitation and coaching. The authors encourage you to seek out and participate in these and other such programs as preparation for group facilitation.

Facilitating a Group

A purposeful group is not just a collection of individuals. A group is an entity in itself. It is a living system with its own physical form, its own personality, its own potential and its own limitations. You are part of a group as an arm or leg is part of a human body. You are not joined physically but you are joined (bonded) emotionally, intuitively, intellectually and spiritually.

And you are part of and bonded to a number of groups—family, household, work, recreation and community.

Being in a group can be threatening for most of us as it brings up our fear of losing our own identity and autonomy. You might be afraid of losing your free will or being dominated by others. Perhaps you don't know what you have to contribute or where your limits are. You might be swayed by the views of others against your better judgment. These fears are real.

As children and teenagers, you are often subjected to powerful peer pressure to conform to a particular group's values and behavior.

Your own family can exert a very controlling form of group pressure: *You must do what we (Mom and Dad) say or be punished.*

A cooperative group can be particularly threatening in this way because everyone is supposed to reach agreement on major decisions.

Will I feel pressured to agree?

Will I be compromised and give in to peer pressure so people will like me or so I don't stand out?

A facilitator needs to be aware of the individual's need for autonomy, of the collective need for cooperation and of the group as a whole system, an organism with a particular culture and personality.

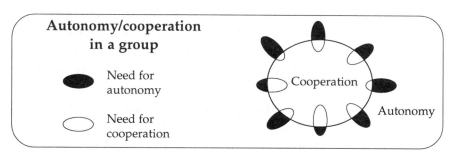

Autonomy/cooperation in a group

Need for autonomy

Need for cooperation

Cooperation

Autonomy

The relationships between group members are also complex and form a web of interaction, each strand with its own unique character.

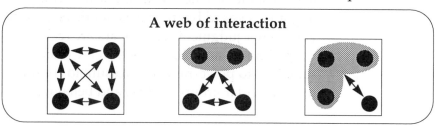

A web of interaction

Being with a group

Being with a group is a development of being with yourself and being with another. Being with a group is *being with yourself and with a number of others*. It is being part of a larger self, part of an organism or entity with its own purpose and personality.

As a facilitator, ask yourself the following questions:

Am I comfortable being with myself and others in this group?

Am I comfortable being part of this group?

Am I comfortable with the way this group works?

Do I know the values of this group?

Am I comfortable with them?

Am I comfortable with the culture and personality of this group?

Is there someone in this group I find particularly upsetting?

Have I done an identity check with that person directly or indirectly (that is, not in his or her presence)? (See Identity Check, Process B7 of the Toolkit, page 151.

Also ask yourself these questions:

Do I want to dominate this group?

Do I feel dominated by this group?

Am I afraid of this group?

Do I know what is best for this group?

Do I have the right process for this group?

Am I an expert on the subject this group is addressing?

Do I like some of the members of this group but not others?

Do I agree with some of the members of this group but not others?

Am I the only person who will work well with this group?

Think about each of these or discuss them with your coach. "Yes" answers to these questions are all good reasons for *not* working with a group.

And consider these questions:

Coming from an attitude of "I don't know," am I committed to empowering this group to achieve its purpose?

Am I committed to taking care of every person in the group and creating a safe environment for all to be fully self-expressed and authentic?

"Yes" answers to these questions are good reasons for working with a group.

Facilitating a group is putting yourself on the edge of the sword

Facilitating a group takes a certain fearlessness (and this includes feeling scared). It takes sufficient awareness of yourself to realize you don't know how to do it (even though you have a toolkit of skills) and a willingness to go with the flow of the group. It requires tapping into the group mind and creativity (which includes challenging the group and halting the flow if it is sabotaging the group purpose).

Group facilitation is moment-by-moment awareness, being awake and in action—awake in the way a hunter stalks a tiger or a mother watches over her newborn infant.

A group facilitator needs:

Self-awareness: being with yourself

Awareness of others: being with others

Commitment to the group fulfilling its purpose

The facilitator's relationship to the group

The facilitator is granted that role by the group. It is a different relationship from that of teacher and class, parent and children, manager and staff, or conductor and orchestra. In these situations most of the responsibility and accountability rests with the teacher, parent, manager and conductor and is to an outside source. The facilitator, however, is responsible and accountable only to the group (and herself or himself).

The role of facilitator is a role of honor and trust given by the group. The group has recognized the importance of the group process and contracts with the facilitator to guide the group process toward the fulfillment of the group purpose.

We trust you to guide the process of our group so that the group can wholeheartedly achieve its purpose.

Starting work with a group

When working with a new group, the facilitator will want to check out the group's expectations of the facilitation role. What the group expects from the facilitator will depend on the members' previous experience with facilitators. Ask the group:

What are your expectations of a facilitator?

You, as facilitator, will also want to share your own values and ways of working with a group and your expectations of the group. Sharing these things means you can be quickly known by the group and it encourages an open atmosphere of sharing in the group.

I will tell you something about myself and my way of working with a group.

This initial checking-out process will reveal whether there are marked differences between the expectations of the group and the facilitator. If there are, they will need to be immediately to determine whether it is appropriate for the group to work with that particular facilitator. This process is usually best carried out in advance by representatives of the group interviewing the facilitator before hiring. For more on this see Chapter 9, Facilitation and the Client.

Guidelines for a facilitator

Group facilitation is the art of guiding the group process toward the agreed objectives. A facilitator guides the process and does not get involved in content. A facilitator intervenes to protect the group process and keep the group on track to fulfill its task.

There is no recipe for a facilitator to follow and there is no one right way to facilitate a group. But here are some guidelines, techniques and tips which you may find useful (these guidelines include material from our book *The Zen of Groups—A Handbook for People Meeting with a Purpose*):

A group is capable of more than any one member thinks

One + one + one + one = 5 or more. This is the equation of synergy. A group is capable of much more than each individual member thinks is possible. You have no idea what you can achieve in a group. Maybe you can achieve almost anything in the world as a group. It may take some ingenuity to discover how you can achieve it. An effective facilitator knows that group members can achieve amazing results and are stopped mainly by baggage from the past. The facilitator is out to tap the energy of the group and tap into the group synergy.

Trust the resources of the group

The facilitator trusts that the group will have the resources to achieve its task and work through any process issues. Trust, in this sense, is an attitude of confidence that the resources are present and will be discovered. The facilitator enables the group to explore and find the resources. This is the way a group becomes empowered. This does not mean that the task will always be fulfilled. It means you don't give up when the going gets tough, even if all group members are wilting.

Honor each group member

Facilitation is about honoring each group member and encouraging full participation while having the group task achieved effectively and efficiently. Always approach group members as capable, aware and fully functioning people who are committed to the group purpose. Even if they are behaving in disruptive ways, always treat them as if they were acting honorably and for the good of the group.

Keep the group space safe

It is important to keep the room or space safe from interruptions and distractions. The facilitator ensures the physical space is safe and guarded from interruptions and intrusion. A group also has an "energetic" space, and the facilitator is aware of this and watches out for it in the same way a mother looks out for a child who may wander unconsciously into danger. On a spiritual level, group space is sacred space.

> **Facilitation is like dancing. If your mind wanders, you miss the rhythm and trip.**

Stand in the group purpose

Always keep in mind the group purpose. It can be useful to have this on a large sheet at each meeting. *Presencing* the group purpose will keep the group on track and grounded and provide you with a place to stand when the group gets distracted or bogged down.

Be adaptable

There is no one technique that will always work at a particular time for the group. It is a matter of choosing, in a particular moment, what to do, whether or not to intervene, and how to intervene. You can plan ahead, but you always need to be ready to adapt to what is happening in the moment.

Remember that beginnings are crucial

Group meetings and workshops have a beginning, a middle and an end. Getting started is like setting out on a journey or laying the foundation of a house. The first part of a group meeting or workshop is crucial to the whole process and time needs to be allowed for the process of starting.

Take everything that occurs as relevant

A facilitator takes everything that is said or done in the group as *group interaction,* including individual exchanges, side comments, and accidental occurrences. For example, if someone falls off his or her chair, that becomes part of the group process rather than an interruption. Some facilitators use outside interruptions as well, like someone coming into the room accidentally.

Work with conflict

A facilitator is comfortable with conflict and always encourages it to be expressed openly. Disagreement is the natural result of different personalities, different views and opinions. If a group is to develop to maturity, it will need to work with conflict, rather than avoid it. Creative conflict resolution can be synergistic, leading to major breakthroughs and forward movement in a group. Remember: don't get tripped up by conflict and don't get involved in the content.

Be awake

Your most important asset as a facilitator is your awareness. Be *awake* and *present* to each moment, moment by moment—listening, looking, sensing—100 percent present. Personal development work, meditation, consciousness-raising, discussion, training and development in experiential learning techniques are all useful ways to develop awareness. Experiment to find ways that work for you.

Be yourself

As a facilitator, you will be most effective when you are being your natural self and allowing your own personality to be expressed. People get permission to be themselves from the way a facilitator behaves—through modeling. If you are stiff and formal, the group tends to be like that. If you are relaxed and self-expressed, the group tends to be like that too. Keep checking to see in what way the group is reflecting you.

Stay clear

This is similar to being awake and present moment by moment. As a facilitator, notice when you get tripped up by your own or others' baggage. When you do get tripped up, note the *trigger* word or phrase (for you to work through later), recover yourself quickly and carry on. Don't take personally, or get drawn into any comment on, ideas or beliefs expressed in the group nor any criticism, no matter how personal. If you get triggered and are unable to recover quickly, use Clearing Yourself when Facilitating, Process B11c of the Toolkit, page 163.

Develop discernment

Make sure your eyes and ears are open all the time. Listen and see without judgment, but with discernment. When is someone tripped up? When is someone asleep, upset, caught in a pattern or triggered? When are people tripping one another up or sabotaging the group? Are they aware of it? Do they want to stop? Who has given up and why? Who is raring to go and frustrated by the inaction of others? Discern when these behaviors are present and if an intervention is necessary.

Get the job done

Always remember you are there to get the job done. Make sure you know the purpose of the group and the desired outcome for the particular meeting you are facilitating. Check how much time the group is prepared to spend on group process issues.

Don't be attached to your own interventions

You may come up with what you think is a brilliant intervention, but if it doesn't work, drop it. The only reason to use an intervention is to keep the group focused, not because you think it is brilliant. Your job is not to show how clever you are.

Use questions and suggestions

Questions and suggestions are the usual way a facilitator intervenes. Avoid giving advice. Say "I suggest . . . " rather than "What you should do is . . ." Also avoid giving the answer to an issue. Your job as facilitator is to guide the process, not to be involved in the content, even if you've got the answer.

Negotiate and contract

A facilitator is an effective negotiator within groups. The structure and framework of meetings and processes are developed through negotiation. Proposals and counter-proposals are encouraged until agreement is reached. Agreement = the contract. Most group decisions—including ground rules, time limits, personal responsibilities, roles, commitment, membership, values, purpose, aims, objectives and evaluation methods—are negotiated.

Be culturally sensitive

Cultural sensitivity is essential for a facilitator. If you are working with people from cultures other than your own, knowledge of their customs, rituals and sensitivities is most important. If you do not have this knowledge, you need to say so and seek advice from people in the group to ensure that cultural sensitivity is honored. Community sensitivities need to be addressed in a similar way. Don't assume—ask.

Improvise

Facilitation is an improvisatory art within an agreed and negotiated structure. In this way, it is like jazz rather than classical music. Don't get stuck doing things a certain way. Remember, there is no one way or technique. Be flexible and stay awake.

Acknowledge and affirm

A facilitator gives frequent acknowledgment and affirmation to a group. Encourage your group to keep going during long or difficult processes by affirming progress and acknowledging completion of tasks. Model the giving of acknowledgment and affirmation. Encourage group members to affirm and acknowledge one another.

Use humor

A sense of humor is a great asset to a facilitator. The use of humor can effectively defuse some tense moments. There is nothing better than a light touch at the appropriate time.

Keep intervention to a minimum

Only intervene in group discussion when it is necessary to interrupt behavior that is:

- ☐ Impeding progress toward fulfilling the task without the agreement of the group.
- ☐ Off track in the discussion and the result of someone having tripped over baggage from the past.
- ☐ Undermining the possibility of group synergy occurring.
- ☐ Physically dangerous.

Monitor the energy level

Monitor the energy level of the group at all times. This is your barometer. Energy is indicated by tone of voice, body posture, eye contact, level of participation and level of activity directed toward the task. Are people awake or asleep? Engaged or disengaged?

The energy of a group will change. At the beginning of a day people often have lots of energy. After lunch they are very often low in energy. Short breaks or active exercises can help keep energy up for longer sessions. For most people, concentration is hard to maintain for longer than 30 to 40 minutes. Keep some active exercises in your repertoire to use when energy is low and the meeting is long (see Tools for Energizing the Group in the toolkit of *The Zen of Groups*).

Seek agreement

A facilitator seeks agreement from everyone and uses collective decision-making processes (consensus) unless there is agreement by everyone to do otherwise. Voting, majority or otherwise, is not a recommended way of reaching a decision in a facilitated group.

When in doubt, check it out

"When in doubt, check it out" is a useful guideline for a facilitator. If you are not clear that everyone is in agreement with a decision or task, ask if everyone agrees. If necessary, request a response from everyone—a yes or a no. Silence does not necessarily mean assent.

If you don't know, say so

If you don't know what to suggest or do when an intervention seems to be needed in a group, say so and ask for suggestions. Someone else may have a good idea, or a suggestion may spark an idea for you. Don't pretend you know everything—nobody does. Trust the group.

Invite feedback

A facilitator invites feedback during and at the end of group meetings. All feedback is useful. Specific comments are more useful than general ones. One feedback technique is the use of rounds of negative and positive comments.

Synergy

Synergy is about tapping into group energy so that group members are able to accomplish more than they thought possible. Tapping into group energy increases dramatically the speed at which a group takes action. Synergy is about flowing and working together harmoniously. It is about coordinated action and being inspired by one another.

How can you tap into this group energy in a conscious way rather than by accident? In everyday life, people usually feel separate from one another. You are an individual and different from everyone else. You like it this way. It is a function of the different baggage you carry, and it keeps you separate from others.

The ability to let go of your baggage, even momentarily, will allow you to identify with and feel for others in a more direct way. In a group, this can be experienced as trust, closeness, peacefulness, understanding, happiness, joy and exhilaration (all aspects of love in its broadest sense). This is what people crave when in groups—unity, acceptance and trust (love).

Increasing group and facilitation skills will open up the pathway to experiencing synergy in your group. Group skills increase the level of cooperation in a group—members begin to listen to one another in a new way, and start to recognize when they are in tune with others. Differences are voiced quickly and worked through. Group members take responsibility for their own baggage and strive to stay clear with one another.

But synergy is not the result of following rules. It is more subtle than that. It is something to value and generate. Force will produce the opposite of synergy—separateness, and the rigid taking and defending of positions.

Synergy is Zen. A facilitator trains to listen for the subtleties of group energy—what will enhance it and what will detract from it. This is the art of facilitation. Developing and using the techniques in a skillful way is the craft.

> **A group is capable of much more than
> each member thinks is possible.**

Some signposts to synergy

We have identified a number of signposts or milestones which may assist your group in finding a pathway to synergy:

Purpose—The group has a clear purpose and group members are committed to it.

Vision—A powerful vision is developed by the group. Building the vision, and recording it in some way—in words, art or music—serve as an ongoing inspiration to group members, particularly when the going gets tough.

Values—Implied in the group purpose and vision will be a number of values. These are teased out by the group and referred to, particularly when making tough decisions.

Clarity—The group clarifies roles and commitments such as membership, ground rules, expectations and limits.

Projects—The group devises projects to achieve its purpose, with clear accountabilities and action plans.

Identity—Group members develop a strong group identity. Trust is developed as group members share themselves honestly with one another. Members honor one another and make allowances for each other's baggage.

Communication—The group finds agreed ways to work through conflict rather than avoid it. Conflict is seen as normal. Feelings are seen as normal. People agree to communicate, even when it's hard.

Learning—Group members increase effectiveness by identifying what they have learned as they go along through group process and project monitoring and evaluation.

Acknowledgment—Group members acknowledge their contributions and the contributions of others to the group.

Celebration—Group members celebrate together the accomplishments of the group.

A group is an entity in itself.

On the Edge of the Sword

The art of intervention

The facilitator's job is to make it easy for the group to achieve its purpose, and to empower the group to tap into its full synergistic potential. The facilitator taps into the power of listening and speaking.

Listening

Listening is the primary skill of facilitation. The quality of your listening will profoundly affect the group. Listening is active, focused and affirming. You listen for the whole group, and for each person in it. You hear where the group has been, where they are going and how they might best get there. You listen for the group purpose, projects and commitments, and the magnificence of each person. You listen to the spoken and unspoken conversation. You listen for what is present and for what is missing. The group is focused and energized through the power of your listening.

Your facilitation also trains the listening of the group through modeling and reminding. As we said in Chapter 3, listening is usually full of assessments and judgments—this is *distressed listening*. What you are developing as a facilitator is *distress-free listening*.

Speaking

Powerful speaking is *whole-body speaking*—the body is centered, the breathing is deep and relaxed, the voice comes from deep in the chest. The voice resonates and projects. It has a ring to it. As a facilitator, you use your voice like a musical instrument. You can use it to direct, encourage, support, calm, inspire and play. Your voice is the authentic expression of your intent as a facilitator. It makes available the whole range of your human expression— from your gentle and vulnerable inner child to your distress-free authority and power.

The speaking of the facilitator is known as *intervention*. The interventions of the facilitator can be described as the strokes of a sword—a sword which engages in a dance with the speaking and listening of the group members, drawing forth cooperation and creativity, probing the group blocks, and disarming the barriers to synergy. As facilitator, you guide the group process and guard against the tendency of participants to trip on their baggage.

How does a facilitator know what to say?

A facilitator doesn't know what to say in advance. You listen for what needs to be spoken to facilitate the group. This is what you speak "in the moment." You become an instrument of the group purpose. You are there for the group. You tap into the higher purpose of the group, whether it is spoken or unsaid. You speak to have the group win and synergy occur.

Facilitation is an improvisatory art. As in swordsmanship and jazz, you can practice the strokes or riffs, watch or listen to other practitioners, and seek to understand the philosophy and values. Facilitation itself can occur only in practice—by being in action.

Intervention training

To assist facilitators in training themselves, the remainder of this chapter lists a variety of interventions in a number of areas. This will give you a feel for the way a facilitator works with a group. Notice how the interventions usually take the form of questions and suggestions.

Use these interventions if you want to but preferably read them for your enlightenment. Consider both the attitude of the facilitator using them (where he or she is coming from/who he or she is being) and the possible response from the group when each is used.

Climate and culture setting

How would you like the seating arranged? How do we want to work in the group?

What roles do you want to cover (facilitator, recorder, time-keeper)? Who would like to take the role of (recorder, timekeeper)?

What ground rules would you like? Any suggestions?

What values are important?

What are the characteristics of your ideal group? Shall we have a brainstorm?

> **Facilitation includes balancing and harmonizing the rhythms of nature.**

What processes for joining and leaving do you want?

What do you not want to see happen in this group?

If you were to be in this group for the next five years, what would you like to be set in place now—processes, rules, guidelines?

Is this group discussion to be confidential to the group? Any exceptions?

Is trust important in the group? Suggest techniques to develop it.

What are your hopes and fears regarding the group? Let's have a round to share these.

Managing time

This session will end at (time). Is everyone in agreement with this? Anyone not?

The breaks will be at . . . and . . . Any problems with these times?

Let's put times beside the agenda items.

How much time will we spend on this issue?

Our time is up. We will stop this discussion now.

How much more time do you propose?

Does everyone agree?

Not all of the group wants to extend the discussion so we will stay with the original time agreed.

It is now time to start again.

Bill, can you please ask people to come back in from the break? We need to get started.

I want us to start in two minutes. Please be ready.

Getting participation

Let's have a round and see what everyone is thinking (or feeling). How about people who haven't spoken so far? What do you think (or feel)?

What do you think, Dale?

What are your feelings about this, Anne?

Let's have a brainstorm. Call out your ideas. Don't censor them. Bill, could you please write the ideas on the whiteboard?

Who'd like to speak first?

Share with your neighbor (the person next to you).

Who would like to share with the whole group?

Now let's go around the whole group. We'll start here.

Remember it's okay to pass or decline.

Who can sum up the (issue/main ideas/areas of difference/where we have gotten to)?

Being present and awake

Does anyone have anything they would like to say to be here (fully present)?

Is anything getting in the way of anyone participating fully in this discussion?

Is anything going on for you Dale? You have become very quiet/look worried/seem upset. Is there anything you would like to say?

Share with your partner any concerns you have about this issue.

Is there anything you would like to share with the group?

Are there any concerns about the group or the process?

The energy is low. Often this indicates there are things that people are holding back. Does anyone have anything they would like to say?

Find someone you feel comfortable with and share something you have been afraid to say in the whole group.

Let's stand up and stretch (swap seats or do an energizing exercise) to get the energy moving.

Let's have a round of things we've been withholding.

What would it take to wake everyone up? Any suggestions?

Here's a joke that might wake everyone up.

Creating a future

What are your hopes and dreams about this?

What can you see developing out of this in the future?

What will this lead to in three years' time?

Imagine yourself in the future (say 10 years from now). What do you see?

Let's do a group visualization exercise and see what's in the future.

Let's pretend we have been traveling in space and arrive back to find that three years have passed. What do you see?

What are we building?

How will your children see this?

What might your children say about this in 10 years' time?

What do you want to end up with (or put in place)?

What are the steps that will lead us into the future?

If we look through the fog, what do we see?

What's the best way this can turn out?

What's the worst thing that can happen?

Drawing out issues

What are the issues here? I'll write them on the whiteboard.

There are several issues within this discussion. Let's draw them out and address them one at a time.

Would someone like to play the role of devil's advocate?

There seems to be an underlying issue here which we are missing. Can anyone identify it?

How do these issues fit together? Can someone put up a model on the board?

What is the key issue here?

Keeping on task

We are getting distracted. Let's get back on task.

Can anyone summarize where we have gotten to?

How can we move this issue forward?

What is the main task?

What steps can we take?

Let's put this new issue on the agenda for later and get back to the first issue.

Who will take responsibility for carrying out this task?

When will it be done?

There are a lot of distractions happening—let's get back to the issue/task.

What do we need to consider or take into account to have this resolved?

Shifting levels

How are people feeling about this issue now?

How is the energy level?

Who has a sense of what is going on in the group?

Is everyone comfortable or do we need a stretch (or a break)?

What do you think about this issue? Let's set up a continuum to get a picture of the range of views.

Who can speak for the higher purpose (or wisdom) of the group?

Anne, could you be the Goddess of Wisdom, and speak to the group?

How would you like to start this session? Would someone suggest a ritual we could adapt for the group?

Let's raise the energy of the group by using this technique.

There seems to be some unpleasant baggage spilling into the group. Can anyone say what it is?

Some people have become very quiet. Can you tell us what is going on for you?

This sounds very rational. What do people feel about it?

This sounds very emotional. What do people think about it?

Cutting through patterned behavior

You have said what you don't want to happen, Bill. Can you tell us what you would like to happen?

Can you propose an alternative, Dale?

This conversation is going around in circles. Let's have a proposal we can work on.

You have made a number of criticisms, Anne. What has tripped you up? What has come up for you?

What is your bottom-line concern, Dale?

Bill, you have had time to put forth your view. Let's hear from someone else.

Please don't interrupt when Dale is speaking.

Can we have one conversation at a time?

Let's have a role play or fish bowl to work on this issue.

Let's separate the person from the issue.

What's not being said

I sense that there is something present here that is not being said. What is it?

There is something going on under the surface. Can someone say what it is?

There is a gremlin in the woodwork. Can someone see it and tell us what it is?

Anne, I sense you are holding back. What do you really want to say?

The unsaid is louder here than the spoken.

There seems to be a lot people are not saying.

There is constipation present in the group. It's time for the crap to hit the fan.

Who can say what's missing here?

Let's have a round on what's missing in this discussion.

How do you account for the (low energy/anger/lack of participation/etc.) in the group? What does it suggest to you?

What do you think is happening here?

Identifying agreement and disagreement

Can someone sum up the agreement already reached? Now we'll check that out with the whole group.

The agreement we seem to have reached is . . . Does everyone agree? The areas of agreement are: (a) . . ., (b) . . ., (c) . . .

The areas of disagreement are: (a) . . ., (b) . . ., (c) . . .
Is this how everyone sees it?

Does this wording (on the board) capture the agreement reached?

We do not have agreement. Let's capture the different perspectives on the whiteboard.

Can you or someone else summarize your perspective?

Who is not happy with this solution?

What would you like changed?

What words would you like added or deleted?

Please say "yes" if you agree, "no" if you don't.

I take it that everyone agrees? (Silence means assent?)

Can you live with this decision?

Thank you for allowing this decision to be reached without using a veto. Would you like your contrary view written down in the records?

> **Peace is an active force, not just an agreement not to harm one another.**

Learning

What did you notice?

Were there any surprises?

How does this connect with what you already understand?

How will you use these ideas?

If you did this again, what would you like to be different?

What have been your major learnings from this (project/workshop/seminar)?

What is the essence of your learnings—in one sentence?

Feedback and acknowledgment

Let's have a round of constructive criticism.

Let's have some feedback on that idea.

Is there any further constructive criticism?

Now let's have positive feedback and acknowledgment.

I acknowledge you, Dale, for . . .

Let's have a round of acknowledgment.

Find someone in the group whose work you appreciate, and go and acknowledge him or her now.

Write down the names of three people in the group you admire and what it is you appreciate about them.

We will write the feedback on the whiteboard in two columns: Constructive criticism/Acknowledgment. Let's have two rounds—the first on constructive criticism and the next on acknowledgment.

I request your feedback on my facilitation. First, constructive criticism, please?

Thank you, I have some useful learning from that. Now for acknowledgment please? Thank you. Yippee!

Completion

What do you need to say to be complete on this?

What do you need to say so that you can move on?

What would you say now if you were never able to be with this group again?

If a bomb was going to explode in two minutes, what do you want to say now?

What would complete this for you?

What is stopping you from being satisfied with the outcome?

Is there anything more you need to say or do?

Is anyone still incomplete?

Is there anything you would like to say after you leave this group? Please say it now.

Problems not shared always get worse.

Working on Different Levels

A group operates on a number of different levels at all times. Group facilitation works with these different levels. This is part of the magic or alchemy of being a facilitator. A facilitator may appear to people in groups as a magician:

How did you pick up on that?

What did you see that caused you to make that suggestion?

When you said that, the group came together.

What did you do that made us all get into action?

Awareness of the different levels develops gradually for the facilitator. It is useful training to practice distinguishing the different levels operating in the group. Here are some notes on the different levels. Explore them. You may come up with some more of your own.

The physical level

The physical level is about people being comfortable and having their physical needs attended to. Care needs to be taken with:

Seating arrangements.

External noise.

Room temperature.

Clean air.

Adequate food and drinks.

Toilet facilities.

Breaks for food, toilet and other physical needs.

Effective lighting.

Resources—whiteboards, videos, as needed.

Special needs—language interpreters, childcare, facilities for the disabled.

The environment needs to suit the function and style of the meeting and the culture of the organization.

Encourage:

Planning for physical needs in advance.

People saying what they need to be comfortable at the beginning of a meeting.

People being on time to start and restart after breaks.

Avoid:

Ignoring participants' physical needs.

Insufficient preparation.

The thinking level

The thinking or intellectual level is the predominant mode used by work and project groups. This level involves:

The sharing of ideas.

The exploration of issues.

Brainstorming.

Creative thinking.

Inspiration.

Analysis.

Critical thinking.

At this level you will notice the words used are:

I think . . .

I've noticed . . .

I understand . . .

My vision is . . .

Can you imagine . . . ?

We need to consider . . .

Through sharing our thoughts, we inspire one another, share visions and create the future. We discover common values and build commitment, recognizing each person's individual contribution. By thinking through and analyzing how, we determine how we can *do things together.*

> **Now I see that, instead of trying to not be overbearing, I can be in a dance.**

Encourage:

Speaking the possibility of the future.

Speaking which moves the conversation forward.

Intentional speaking—*This will be.*

Sharing ideas—not holding back.

Full participation.

Mining the gold (listening for people's magnificence).

Diversity of ideas.

Avoid:

Withholding.

Thinking small.

Domination by a few.

Complaining and negative speaking.

Discussion that doesn't go anywhere.

Criticizing personalities.

The emotional level

The emotional level is the level of feelings where we are:

Sharing experiences.

Sharing feelings.

Expressing feelings (grief, anger, fear, love, enthusiasm).

At this level the words used will be:

I feel . . .

I care . . .

I'm concerned . . .

We can access speaking from the heart—authentic speaking that moves others, finds empathy with them and arouses their feelings.

Encourage:

Sharing from the heart.

Participants owning their own distress.

Listening for one another's magnificence.

The presence of love.

Trust.

Empathy and compassion.

Caring for the planet.

Avoid:

People shutting down their feelings.

Shutting down the expression of feelings by others.

Filling up the silence.

Distress projected onto others (blaming and fault finding).

The intuitive level

This is speaking which encapsulates the essence and finds the common chord, intuiting what is going on for people. Words used will be:

I sense that . . .

There is something not quite right here

There is something wrong here.

We are onto something—I've almost got it.

Intuitive speaking is in tune with the group—speaking which expresses what is present but unsaid.

Encourage:

Listening for the whole group.

Listening for what needs to be said.

Speaking the unsayable.

Recognition of the group wisdom.

Avoid:

Ignoring the unspoken upset.

Ignoring the group wisdom.

Pretending the distress will go away.

The energy level

This is a nonverbal level where you pick up or sense the energy by observing participants' behavior, posture, tone and animation of voices, attentiveness, "vibes." At this level, you appreciate where people are at—how awake the group is; how attuned and focused it is.

You need to be able to move the energy level from low to high or vice versa.

Encourage:

Awareness of energy levels by participants.

Recognition of key energy points and shifts.

Recognizing times to shift the energy level.

Avoid:

Ignoring the group energy.

The ritual or spiritual level

The ritual level is where you tap into the higher purpose of the group, the fine energy of the higher consciousness, the *God* energy. This is done by the use of music, dance, art, meditation and ritual to invoke the higher (spiritual) energies—compassion, love, planetary consciousness, universal love and joy, essence or spirit of peace.

Encourage:

Development of group rituals by the group.

Fun, joy and self-expression.

Practices that deepen the group experience.

Group rituals that express the essence of the group.

Simple, powerful practices.

Embracing cultural diversity.

Inclusion of all.

Discourage:

Superimposing rituals designed by others.

Rituals that don't inspire everyone.

Rituals that have become meaningless or boring.

The synergistic level

This is the level of *transformation*, of heightened awareness when the group is at one—aligned, attuned and integrated. This is the level at which the group recognizes itself as an organism with one mind. Each group member has direct access to this mind and is able to speak it. The energy of the group is palpable and there is a clarity, spaciousness and timelessness. These are the magic experiences you will always remember and treasure—and everyone in the group will feel them.

At this level, group members:

Have "aha" experiences as others say what they were about to say or think.

Speak with voices that have changed in quality and seem to resonate.

Feel in tune and at one with the group.

Drop their judgments of others.

Feel that suddenly there is plenty of time even though an issue is urgent.

Notice others in a new way.

Feel guided or supported by a higher self.

Encourage:

Alignment with the group purpose.

Clearing.

Attunement.

Spontaneity.

Lightness and humor.

Creativity.

Stretching beyond usual limitations.

Not stopping.

Sharing at a deep level.

Appreciation.

Discourage:

Discounting of self and others.

Cynicism.

Negativity.

Small-mindedness.

Members hanging onto positions or baggage.

Noticing the levels

A facilitator observes the group at a number of levels and notices when a level change will forward the group purpose. Noticing the levels can be accessed through:

Listening to the sound, tone, pitch and speed of participants' speaking.

Watching body movements, facial expressions, body language.

Listening to the length and quality of silences.

Sensing energy changes.

Sensing the presence of love and the higher energies.

After noticing the levels, it is helpful for a facilitator to share these experiences with another facilitator to develop a fuller and more developed sense of the subtleties involved. Ask one another

"What did you see or notice?" and share your experiences. You may have similar or different experiences. Just mention them; don't try to make one another right or wrong. Keep sharing experiences and see if there is some agreement.

Working with the levels

Working with or drawing attention to a number of levels is a skill a facilitator needs to develop. The simplest way to develop this skill is through:

Noticing the different levels.

Sharing your observation with the group.

Gaining the group's agreement to shift level.

Using an appropriate technique or process to highlight a level.

Model being present on the different levels (for example, speaking from the heart will encourage participants to do the same).

Example

*The group has been meeting for an hour. A discussion has gotten bogged down and is going nowhere. People are looking tired and are slumped in their chairs. Dale is the facilitator. She notices that the group is stuck in their heads (**thinking level**) and that the energy is low (**energy level**).*

*She shares her observation with the group, and invites them to stand up and stretch for two minutes to increase the energy (**physical level**). The group agrees to do this. After the break, she invites them to have a round, each sharing their feelings about the issue (**emotional level**) for two minutes.*

The comfort level of the facilitator will determine the degree to which the levels can be explored by the group. The facilitator's ease will give participants permission to explore the levels and build the trust and safety for exploration to occur. As the group opens up to the levels, participants enter a new way of relating with one another.

If you want group effectiveness and synergy, you need to know you can't get there without taking care of the multi-dimensional nature of the group. It's like an iceberg—probably 90 percent of what is really going on is submerged and will go unnoticed unless the facilitator or a participant draws attention to it, bringing it to the consciousness of the group as a whole.

The facilitator is always looking for the balance which will allow each group to become synergistic. There will be a workable balance of levels for each group for full effectiveness.

Most work groups tend to operate well at the thinking level, but are unaware of other levels. A group that operates only on the thinking level will not bond. Bonding requires a shift to the emotional level. Many work groups are unaware of the necessity to bond as a group if they are to be effective. Sports team are often more aware of the importance of emotional bonding, which they often do by socializing after the game.

A group whose purpose requires creativity (design, innovation, development, envisioning) will need to raise its awareness of and tap into the intuitive level to fully access the group creativity.

> **A group that operates only on the thinking level will not bond. Bonding requires a shift to the emotional level.**

7 Getting to Agreement

The decision-making model which underpins cooperacy is known as *collective* (or *consensus*) *decision-making*.

Collective decision-making is based on an *agreement to reach agreement* by the whole group on all decisions made. All group members have the right to choose to participate or not in all decisions. Such agreements will vary and may include some of the following:

- ☐ Everyone is actively involved in all decisions.
- ☐ Those directly affected by a decision are involved in the decision. (All group members agree in advance what "directly affected" means.)
- ☐ All disagreements must be worked through before action is taken; or
- ☐ Disagreements can be noted and not hold up action if all group members agree to this for a specific decision (agree to disagree).
- ☐ The whole group agrees to give authority to make decisions, within agreed limits, to individuals or subgroups (that is, to delegate).

Collective decision-making draws out the collective wisdom of the group and encourages each group member to own all decisions made. Collective decision-making may take time at first but, with practice, can be quick. And this form of decision-making allows for synergy to occur.

Collective decision-making model

1. When group agreement is needed, request proposals from the group. All proposals are written down without alteration or debate.

2. Ask each group member to indicate the proposal which is the closest to his or her view. Mark each preference with a check. After everyone has spoken, remove or cross out proposals which have no support.

3. Provide an opportunity (such as a round) for each person to speak briefly about his or her preference or to suggest modifications. Add modifications to each proposal, using a different colored pen. Erase checks, because the group members are going to choose again.

4. Encourage people to take a new and fresh look at the proposals. Check each person's preferences again. Add new check marks.

5. Check for agreement. There may be full or partial agreement at this stage. Mark the agreement by circling or underlining the agreed words. Erase or cross out proposals and modifications which are not now supported.

Rule of thumb: Those directly affected by a decision need to be able to participate in the decision-making.

6. If agreement has not been reached, request new proposals or modifications which will capture the wisdom of the group and meet with general agreement. Record these.

7. Repeat steps 5 and 6 if necessary.

8. If a decision is being held up by disagreement from one or two people, ask the dissenters to propose a solution. (This helps them to remain proactive.) Also, check with them to see if they are directly affected by the outcome. If not, see if they will allow the decision to be made anyway.

9. When agreement has been reached, check that everyone is actively in agreement. A round in which each person says "yes" or "no" is useful for this. Do not assume silence means assent.

Barriers to reaching agreement

The major fear that many people have about cooperative groups is in the area of decision-making.

How can you get everyone to agree? It will take too long. It will waste too much time.

Collective decision-making can take longer than majority decision-making to actually reach a decision, but the decisions "stick" and are often put into action more quickly because they have been agreed to by the whole group. Often a lot of time is spent before a majority decision-making meeting by factions canvassing for votes—and the decision-making is taken out of the arena of the meeting.

With collective decision-making, this time is spent in the meeting and everyone is involved. Majority decision-making may be shorter in the process at the meeting, but decisions often are not implemented or may even be sabotaged. And time is often wasted because these decisions have to be made again. Thus collective decision-making is often shorter in the long run. As your collective decision-making skills improve, the time taken to make decisions will decrease.

There are a number of barriers to reaching agreement. The facilitator must become aware of them and learn how to dismantle them.

Making one another wrong

This comes from a failure to recognize that your world is different from another's world—the "I'm okay, you're not okay" approach which we all fall into at times. *Your opinion is different from mine, therefore it must be wrong.* Getting stuck in "I'm right and you're wrong" impedes reaching agreement.

Dismantle this barrier by reminding participants that both or all points of view are valid. Remind participants of their common purpose and values, and ask them and others in the group to suggest a number of alternative solutions which can then be explored. Brainstorming is a useful technique here.

Not being proactive

This is when participants get stuck and can't or won't think of any alternative solutions. They will usually also be stuck in "making one another wrong" mode.

Dismantle this barrier by reminding participants that "every problem holds its own solution" and affirm that they can come up with an agreement everyone can support. A short break or a physical exercise such as changing seating positions can be useful here to impact the negative energy and stuckness.

I have nothing to contribute

This may be the thought pattern of some group members, who then stop themselves from taking part in decision-making processes.

Dismantle this barrier by reminding the group that *everyone* has something to contribute and the people who are contributing the least to the discussion are likely to be the ones who can contribute the most to the decision-making process. Affirm and write down on sheets of paper or a whiteboard all contributions, no matter whether they initially seem unhelpful or off track.

Also check your own listening. Are you listening more generously to some members of the group than others? Why do some members feel they have nothing to contribute?

Getting stuck on one particular outcome

This is called "getting positional" and is similar to making one another wrong. Some participants may be so attached to their solution that they can't or won't let go of it. They become like a dog with a bone and are unwilling or unable to let go.

Dismantle this barrier by allowing the "attached" participant(s) to have uninterrupted time to explain their proposal. Encourage everyone to give it their full attention and to listen generously. Allow them to take as much time as they like without any interruptions. This can be followed by questions for clarification, not argument (be rigorous about this) and then a round in which people indicate agreement, disagreement or part agreement (without discussion or argument).

If there is disagreement or part agreement, request that the "attached" participants put their solution on hold while everyone brainstorms alternative solutions. Look to see how any part agreement reached can be noted and incorporated into other proposals.

Negative and stuck energy

People have become negative or resigned, have stopped contributing, and have given up.

Dismantle this barrier by calling a short break, a stretch, physical exercise or energizer such as someone telling a joke. Don't resume the decision-making process until the energy has shifted. Make sure there is sufficient fresh air in the room and that people are not hungry. There could be physical reasons for low energy. If there is no physical reason, the group may need a clearing session or an opportunity to recreate the group vision.

Cheap closure

Everyone seems to agree and then the decision is challenged again or people are reacting to one another or the facilitator.

Dismantle this barrier by checking the decision again and requesting each person say "yes" or "no" to it as a round.

Note: Do not fall into the trap of assuming silence means assent and rush through decisions without checking them out in an active way.

Not taking responsibility

The group has agreed on a particular course of action, but no one is willing to commit to the individual actions required to carry out the decision.

Dismantle this barrier by challenging the decision. People may be coming from we "should" do this rather than from a genuine commitment. Or it may be personally risky or threatening to carry out the decision (as in a protest group deciding on direct action). If people are still unwilling to commit to action after consideration, request that the group revoke the decision.

> **Do not assume silence means assent.**

Cutting Through

This chapter covers a number of conflict-related issues. These are sabotage, scapegoating, factions, groupthink and challenges.

Conflict

First, a few general comments about conflict. Conflict in groups is normal and inevitable. Conflict can range from mild disagreement to angry outbursts. Few groups, however, would find physical violence acceptable.

Much conflict can be prevented by attending to group-maintenance issues such as ground rules, decision-making processes and record-keeping. When conflict does occur, and it will, it is best handled by attending to it at once. If you do not attend to conflict, it will escalate and lead to resentment, lack of cooperation, lack of energy, people avoiding one another, indirect attacks and subversion in the group.

A highly creative group or an issues-related group is likely to have a higher degree of conflict than some others. Lack of any conflict in a group may indicate apathy, lack of interest, boredom, people feeling unsafe to share, and low self-esteem of group members.

Working through and resolving conflict calls for sensitive and creative facilitation. The art is in knowing when to intervene and when to suggest a process to assist the group. And there is no right answer—each facilitator will intervene differently.

Approach conflict as a normal part of any group. Trust that the group can work it through and that each person has an important role to play in this. If you as facilitator take this approach, and treat each group member with honor and respect, it will reduce the likelihood of group members feeling hurt or damaged by the conflict.

Our other book, *The Zen of Groups*, has a good section on conflict generally and also a range of processes to use for resolving conflict. In this and the following chapter we focus on a number of specific areas where conflict occurs.

Sabotage

This section is about how to recognize sabotage and what the facilitator can do about it.

Sabotage is behavior which undermines the group fulfilling its purpose. Sabotage happens often in a group, usually at an unconscious level, but sometimes at a conscious level. It is usually connected with one or more group members acting out their individual distress in the group by projecting it onto other people who, in turn, get tripped up by their own baggage.

Example 1:
Bill sometimes falls into a "victim" behavior pattern which developed from experiences in his early childhood. He took on a number of tasks in the group but has not fulfilled them by the time agreed. Other members

of the group comment on his not keeping his commitment. Bill reacts as a victim and says the group is picking on him and that they don't understand the pressures he is under. He blows his nose and looks dejected (like a little boy). Group members feel sorry for him, apologize and offer to take on some of his work. In reality, Bill is able to handle the workload and has given other tasks priority.

What is the sabotage here? The group is in victim/rescuer mode—patterned behavior which will interfere with the effective functioning of the group. The facilitator seeks to uncover the sabotage and lead the group through a process to work through the issues. The facilitator uncovers what is really going on and:

- ☐ Clarifies Bill's promise and what got in the way of its being fulfilled.
- ☐ Requests that he recommit to have the tasks done by a certain time or, if he is unable to do this, to revoke his promise.
- ☐ Encourages other group members to support Bill as he sorts out the issue himself, and not to get tripped up by their own "rescuer" patterns, which will only reinforce Bill's using his "victim" pattern.

Example 2:

A decision needs to be made in the group. All but one person have reached consensus. Dale has been feeling angry with several members of the group because her two latest ideas were criticized and not accepted. She wants to punish the group and, although she does not have a particular interest in this specific issue, she knows the group requires agreement by everyone. She refuses to agree or to propose an alternative that might be acceptable to others. She abuses some group members when they challenge her and request her cooperation. Then she walks out of the room, slamming the door. Dale is consciously sabotaging the group.

The issues for the facilitator in this example of conscious sabotage are:

☐ Dale's feelings of anger and alienation related to the earlier incidents. This is unfinished business which needs to be attended to.
☐ Dale's commitment to the group, the group purpose and to reaching agreement are now in question and need to be addressed.
☐ What upset is now present for the other group members and how this can be worked through?
☐ What processes can be put in place to address the above issues?

In this example, a facilitator would intervene before the walkout occurred and, with a series of questions, establish what is going on for Dale.

What's going on for you, Dale?
(Encourage Dale to verbalize her feelings.)

What happened before that you are feeling angry/hurt now?
(Establish when the upset occurred and what happened.)

What can you say or do now to complete this for yourself?

How are other people in the group feeling?
(Establish how other people are feeling and to what extent they are also triggered.)

Sabotage is usually about someone feeling powerless to influence what is happening in the present and becoming triggered back into earlier incidents of powerlessness—often to do with early childhood.

Soon after it's first noticed, it is useful for the facilitator to initiate a discussion on sabotage and how it shows up in a group. Each individual has ways of sabotaging himself or herself. In a group, these patterns are often projected onto the whole group by each individual. We act out our own patterns through others. We create our own dramas. When our dramas are similar or complementary, it is easy for the group to become activated and upset.

When these situations arise, the facilitator will encourage each person to own his or her own feelings:

> *This is happening (description), I am feeling upset/angry/hurt/sad (owning the feelings) and I request that (specific request for action)*

These are the skills of assertion. The facilitator can introduce these skills as needed and encourage the group to use them. They can also reinforce and acknowledge assertive behavior which does occur. See Uncovering Sabotage Patterns, Process B10 of the Toolkit, page 155.

As the facilitator, you also need to beware of your own sabotage patterns and how you may sabotage groups you are facilitating. By getting to know your own patterns, you will be better able to defuse them.

Blaming and scapegoating

Scapegoating happens in all kinds of groups—families, children's peer groups, work groups and recreational groups. Remember the black sheep who is criticized by everyone in the family?

Scapegoating occurs when one person is consistently blamed for things going wrong. It involves blaming and agreement between group members to keep doing this. This agreement will usually be unconscious and the group will appear to be acting on automatic pilot when it gets into this behavior.

The basis of scapegoating is powerlessness and lack of self-esteem in the blamers, which leads to fault finding and needing someone to blame: *I'm not okay so you're not okay either* behavior. This comes from thinking that, when something goes wrong, there needs to be someone at fault, someone to be blamed. Most of us get this message as small children and tend to act it out all our lives: *Something's wrong. Who's to blame?* go together in the same breath.

In families, children often feel powerless and at the mercy of their parents—they are often punished or reprimanded without understanding why. The child who is told he or she is bad will believe it. The child will feel hurt and angry and will try to understand what is going on. He or she may act out these feelings in play with toys or with aggressive behavior towards other children who are smaller or weaker. He or she may play that the doll or other child has done something wrong and needs to be punished.

So the blamed child becomes the blamer, and the behavior is learned and acted on automatically as the child grows up.

Scapegoating is a persistent version of this, involving the victimization of a particular person over a period of time by a group. Scapegoating always fails to honor the person and their humanity. It is damaging and dangerous.

It is a way of avoiding responsibility. *If I focus attention on you, maybe people won't notice my shortcomings.* Have you ever felt a sense of relief when someone else is being blamed? *Thank goodness it's not me.*

Scapegoating also occurs in reverse. Staff may scapegoat the boss or the company in an effort to diminish their power and the staff's own sense of powerlessness. This happens in families when, for example, mom and the kids gang up against dad. This can be open or covert, conscious or unconscious.

The facilitator needs to interrupt blaming and scapegoating as soon as it occurs. With blaming, encourage participants to acknowledge their own feelings, describe the behavior they don't like in another and make a request.

I feel angry when you keep arriving late to our meetings. It disrupts the meeting and wastes time. I request you come on time.

With scapegoating—an accumulation of blaming which has not been attended to—there is always a history (a number of incidents over time), and this needs to be explored and worked through with the group. Have the group share, possibly in rounds:

What has happened in the past that has you assume that (name of person) has got it wrong again?

What really happened and what expectations weren't fulfilled?

What does each group member need to say about it?

What feelings have not been expressed and owned?

I felt angry when . . .

I feel hurt when . . .

Keep the group sharing until everyone has said all they have to say (is complete) and the poison has been drained. Usually scapegoating is a cover-up for widespread feelings of inadequacy and powerlessness in the group. It may take some careful digging and encouragement to get through to the underlying issues.

When a culture of expressing feelings and making clear requests (assertive behavior) is established in the group, blaming and scapegoating will diminish.

Blaming and scapegoating will also diminish when acknowledgment is occurring in the group. A regular process for acknowledging and appreciating one another establishes that everyone is valuable and worthy of respect. See also Group Clearing, Process B11b in the Toolkit, page 161.

Group factions

Related to blaming and scapegoating are the formation of fixed alliances or factions in groups. Factions are the norm within majority decision-making structures (democracy). Where decision-making is dependent on majority vote, factions have the appeal of cutting down on discussion, and allow for quick and easy decision-making. At its extreme, block voting of political parties makes parliamentary decision-making into a formality—there is almost no effort made toward distilling the collective wisdom.

Factions are another version of "us" and "them" thinking. Usually personalities quickly become intertwined with differing beliefs, values and points of view. *We disagree with others' beliefs.* See My World, Your World, Process B3 of the Toolkit, page 144, and Living in different worlds, Chapter 3, page 21. It is only a small step to this becoming: *We dislike you as personalities.* This is getting back to "us" and "them" thinking, with a similar outcome to blaming and scapegoating, though now the sides may be more even.

Cooperacy, with its collective decision-making, cuts through the formation of group factions. Factions lose their usefulness in collective decision-making and become counterproductive to reaching consensus when the whole group wisdom is being sought and listened for. Factions get in the way of the autonomy-cooperation polarity that is the basis of cooperacy.

Groupthink

On an intergroup level, "us" and "them" behavior is expressed through the phenomenon of *groupthink* . When a group has been going a while and has established its identity, what is likely to emerge is a tendency to think of itself as not only special, but better. Our group is *the best* and *right*; your group is *lacking* and *wrong*.

Being in the group feels good and more powerful than being alone and feeling scared and powerless. Being in a group fulfills our need for belonging and identity. On a large scale, this bonding and identifying becomes community, culture, race and nationalism.

The danger arises not from being different and special (unique), but from believing that different is also better. We all indulge in this in sports, particularly on a national level. We believe our sports teams should win and need someone (or something) to blame if they don't—the wrong players or coach were selected, the referee, the weather, the cheating of the opponents. Our pride is at stake and (we imagine) our own personal sense of worth.

The "isms"—sexism, heterosexism, racism, ageism, adultism, and so on —are all about this kind of right/wrong, member/non-member, good/bad interpretation of the world through the eyes of group identity.

Group exclusivity is a result of the unconscious leap from different to better. It fails to recognize our own and others' full humanity. It is a cruel joke which can only backfire because it must mean ultimately that our group is disconnected and alone.

Groupthink is this kind of unconscious behavior in the group. Group members start to adopt an attitude of "the group is this or that and thinks this or that" without taking the time or energy to think individual issues through freshly. Groupthink is automatic and unconscious behavior. And it permeates the whole world. We are all subject to it.

The facilitator will alert the group to any tendency to become automatic and unconscious, and encourage the group to stay awake and aware. *Different in some ways, yes. Better—never.* The way to bridge the gap between groups is to establish commonality of values, purpose, vision and shared experiences. Full humanity covers the whole range of human emotions including love, joy, sadness and loss. Consciousness leads us towards one another, unconsciousness leads us away.

Challenges within the group

Challenging one another within the group is an important skill for both group members and the facilitator. Here is a situation where a challenge is useful:

> *Anne is part of a six-person support group. She is very verbal and tends to dominate all the conversation. She can't seem to stop herself from taking over. She believes her issues are more urgent and more difficult than those of the others, and that she really needs the support and advice of the group. Gradually, the other group members start to switch off when she speaks. They feel increasingly angry with her domination but don't want to hurt her feelings by saying how angry they are.*

Often, groups gradually fall apart rather than challenge a dominating member. There is an unconscious commitment in our culture to be nice at all costs. A challenge to Anne is appropriate here. A group member can initiate a challenge:

> *I feel annoyed, Anne, that you are taking up so much group time. I want more time and I also want other group members to have more equal time. How do other people feel?*

A challenge like this, if handled sensitively, can move the group to greater maturity. The facilitator needs to set up a process, such as a round, which will enable a level of trust and safety to be maintained so the behavior is challenged rather than the person. It is important to keep the process going until all have expressed their feelings and concerns. Anne must have the opportunity to respond at the end of the round to express her feelings and concerns and what she has learned about her own behavior.

When each group member has shared, the facilitator can suggest putting some practices in place to avoid the situation arising again. Practices could include:

- ☐ An agreed time slot for each person to express his or her issues and to get contributions and coaching from others.
- ☐ An agreement that people will take responsibility for their own feelings and challenge one another quickly rather than bottle things up.
- ☐ A round of feedback at the end of each session to clear any issues which have arisen.

Often the need for a challenge within the group will emerge in discussion outside the group. Members will start to comment to one another about a person's behavior and there will be some agreement about the problem. We could criticize this kind of complaining, but we often need to verbalize our thoughts before we know what we think. Outside-the-group discussion gives members an opportunity to clarify their own feelings and perceptions without taking up group time. If there is agreement from others, then we feel more powerful and able to express ourselves in the group—we know there is some support.

However, a more powerful and empowering challenge is one which is made spontaneously in the group:

I feel . . . when you . . . (description of action). Can we discuss this? I'd like to know if other people feel the same way.

This kind of challenge is more high-risk than a challenge based on prior agreement, because the challenger is allowing himself or herself to be vulnerable by expressing his or her feelings. There may be no agreement and the challenger may feel foolish. Nevertheless, this kind of challenge happens often in high-trust groups, where people are encouraged to express and work through their concerns as quickly as possible. Although group members may find it scary at first, the encouragement of spontaneous challenging is a sign of a more mature group.

When a challenge occurs the facilitator will consider:

☐ Which process or technique will be used to work through the issue?

☐ What feelings are present in the group and how intense are they? If they are very intense, the facilitator will want the group to work through the issue as soon as possible.

☐ Can time be made available? Check this out with the group.

☐ What is not being said? Underlying concerns and feelings need to be brought out into the open.

☐ Who is (are) the most powerless person(s) in this situation? Do they need support, and how can this be provided?

☐ Who is the most triggered in the conversation, and by what past incidents within the group? Do these incidents need to be identified and worked through individually?

☐ Have people been triggered back into past incidents that have no direct connection with the group? If there are incidents from early childhood or from other groups, the individuals may need to be reminded to take responsibility for them.

Challenging the group

Sometimes it is useful for the facilitator to challenge the whole group. Some situations where you may want to challenge the group are:

☐ There is underlying conflict which is coming to the surface as indirect attacks.

☐ The energy is low (and you sense it is because people are withholding).

- Scapegoating is occurring.
- The group keeps getting off track and is lacking intentionality.
- The group is in groupthink mode, complaining about others and making them wrong.
- The group is getting into patterned (unconscious) behavior.
- The group is bogged down in detail and has lost sight of the vision.
- The group seems to lack commitment to reach agreement.

You, as facilitator, may first respond by drawing attention to what is happening, encouraging the group to be conscious of it and restating the purpose of the meeting. Then you may suggest a process or technique to move the group on.

What seems to be happening in the group is . . .

The purpose of this meeting is to . . .

What we can do to interrupt this pattern is . . . Do you agree?

If the group does not respond at first, you may need to repeat the process or interrupt the pattern by:

- Calling a short break.
- Asking people to stand up and stretch.
- Sharing in pairs.
- Having a round of acknowledgments.
- Choosing a trust-building exercise.

Challenges to the facilitator

One of the fears of a new facilitator is of being challenged by the group. Challenges can come in different forms, direct and indirect. Here are some examples of challenges you might meet:

Direct:

This process is not working.

You are too directive or not directive enough.

Your style doesn't suit our group.

Your interventions are inappropriate.

You are upsetting me or another member of the group.

You are too inexperienced for this group.

Indirect:

People slow to respond to suggestions.

People arriving back late from breaks (often).

People talking among themselves.

People ignoring the facilitator.

A group member taking over the role of the facilitator
without agreement.

Challenges to the facilitator are valid and need to be attended to immediately. Don't pretend it isn't happening. Listen to the challenge and, if unsure, ask it to be restated. Then state it back to the group:

Bill, you feel that this process is not working

Check out the concern with the rest of the group:

Do others agree with this?

If everyone agrees, stop the process and suggest another, or ask for suggestions. If there is no quick consensus, suggest the process continue and be evaluated later in the meeting. Ask Bill if he accepts this. If he declines, ask him to make a specific request of you (as the facilitator) or the group. He may be tripped up by baggage.

If challenges continue, stop the group and request that the whole group consider the issue. Remind them that a facilitator can only work with the agreement of the group.

> *There have been several challenges to my facilitation at this meeting. I can only fulfill this role with the group's agreement. Let's have a round on what isn't working for each person. Could someone record the comments on the whiteboard as I want to listen carefully.*

When the concerns are listed, thank the group for being frank and honest. Group the concerns and then address each one in turn. You may either make suggestions or request suggestions from the group.

If a concern is unclear, ask for clarification or ask if someone could make a specific request. You may, of course, accept or decline the request.

If the concern is general, suggest that you continue until the end of the meeting and that the group considers your continuing role as part of the agenda. Request that another person facilitates this discussion.

No facilitator can work effectively with all groups. Avoid becoming defensive. The group has the right to challenge you and request another facilitator. Retain your dignity. You are okay and so are they. One group's rejection does not mean you are not an effective facilitator.

It helps to take the attitude that you are always in training and are willing to increase your skills. Usually it works to accept the criticism and to be willing to alter specific behavior. In fact, a group will respect you for this and their trust in you will be enhanced.

The encouragement of spontaneous challenging is a sign of a mature group.

Facilitation and the Client

When you are approached to facilitate a group process you can:

- ☐ Already be a member of the group.
- ☐ Be a member of the same organization but not in the group itself.
- ☐ Be an outside facilitator.

There are some issues specific to each situation and some issues common to all. There is some overlap so we suggest you read and consider all the points.

Facilitator already in the group

If you are already a member of a group and are asked to facilitate it, you will need to clarify for yourself and the group how this will work.

Not involved in content

As the facilitator, you will be guiding the process and will not be involved in the content of the group session(s). It doesn't work to pop in and out of the facilitator's role, trying to take part in the decision-making as well as facilitating.

You will need to consider whether you are prepared to forgo your involvement in the content of the group deliberations and whether you will be able to accept any group decisions, particularly if you disagree with them.

Neutrality

You will need to check carefully with the whole group to ensure that every member can accept you as the facilitator. If you have voiced strong opinions within the group or are associated with a particular faction, it may be difficult for some members to accept your ability to be neutral. You will need to check this out carefully and ensure that every group member accepts your taking on this role.

You might want to design a process which can be invoked if concerns about your neutrality arise in the group. A member of the group with a different perspective may be assigned the role of monitoring your neutrality and giving you feedback during or at the end of each session.

Rotating the role of facilitator

The group may want to rotate the role of facilitator among a number of people who have facilitation skills. Each group meeting could have a facilitator assigned in advance, with room for renegotiation if issues of particular interest to individual facilitators are on the agenda.

Rotating the role of facilitator is a useful way for a number (or all) group members to develop facilitation skills. The group also needs to consider its role in training and developing facilitation skills among its members. A group in which all group members are trained in facilitation is very powerful. On the other hand, weak facilitation can hold up the work of the group. It can lead to frustration and lack of energy in the group.

A middle way could be for the group to encourage all members to undertake basic training in facilitation skills before they facilitate the group.

Facilitator within the same organization but not the group

If you work within the same organization but are not part of the group wanting a facilitator, you will need to check out your appropriateness with the whole group.

Confidentiality
You will need to check with the group on their need for confidentiality, and if it applies to content only or to content and process. Assume that content is confidential anyway, but checking is important as the group members may not have an explicit confidentiality agreement (it may be assumed), and you need to protect yourself from any future information leaks which may occur from group members. Be very scrupulous about confidentiality yourself. Your integrity as a facilitator will depend on this.

The group may also want the processes they use kept confidential. Check this out carefully and also negotiate a confidentiality agreement for the whole group.

Power relationships
If you are much more senior in the organization than all or some of the people you are facilitating, this could lead to an unequal amount of power being attributed to you, and the group becoming inhibited and mistrustful of your facilitation. The role of facilitator has considerable power. A facilitator who also has positional power is probably not the best person to facilitate a group. Check this out carefully and be sensitive to the concerns of group members. You may prefer to decline the facilitator's role.

Alternatively, you may have much less positional power than many or all in the group. Group members may have the power to fire you or you may need their support to gain promotion. Check with yourself. Will you be powerful enough to challenge each and every group member if you consider they are sabotaging the group? If not, you will not be the right person to facilitate this group. You need to be fearlessly for the group achieving their objectives. If unsure, discuss your fears with the whole group and get their consent for you to challenge them. You can then refer back to this consent if things get sticky later.

It is useful to record the consent in the minutes of the meeting. Usually getting the group consent is sufficient to give permission to the facilitator. (It is really about giving yourself permission.)

Outside facilitator

As an outside facilitator, you will need to get clear on a number of issues, the first of which is: Who is the client? When you are asked to facilitate a group it is first necessary to identify the client. You may not always be clear who you are really working for.

Is the person who approached you the client?

Is the senior person in the group the client?

Is the whole group the client?

Check carefully with the initial contact person to clarify who the client is. For example, you may be approached by someone from management services or personnel to facilitate a planning session for a business unit within a large company. Ask to speak to the manager of the business unit and negotiate the required outcomes with that person, not the management services person. If at all possible, arrange a meeting with the manager.

Always ask these questions:

Who is my client—to whom am I accountable?

Who will negotiate the required outcomes with me?

Has the group agreed to accept me as the facilitator?

When facilitating a community group, meet with two or three representatives beforehand to check out the background of the group and to negotiate the outcomes.

Checking for match between facilitator and group

At the preliminary meeting, check for a suitable match between the group and yourself as the facilitator.

What is the background of the group?

The kinds of questions you might ask are:

Is the group from the business, public or community sector?

What kind of organization—professional, service or grass roots?

What is the size of the organization—large or small, and at what level is the group within the organization?

If local or central government, are politicians involved?

How did you hear about me?

It is helpful to you to know whther this was by referral from a previous client or participant, through an advertisement, professional association or colleague.

Do my values and experience match with the group goals and values?

It is helpful to have written promotional material about yourself or your business for potential clients. This material can include a statement of your own philosophy, values and experience. It is also helpful to include a photograph.

What is the age, sex, sexual orientation and ethnic mix of the group?

Are issues likely to arise around any of these concerning your ability as facilitator? Does the group know enough about your facilitation style and methods? Has the group used a facilitator before? An outside facilitator or an internal facilitator?

Would the contacts like to talk with a previous client of a similar kind to check out your suitability for the group? It is good practice to offer this opportunity to new clients.

Has the whole group been consulted and has it agreed to your facilitation? Or have you been approached by one faction without consultation with the whole group. (This has happened to us.)

Negotiating the contract

What is the request?

What is the nature of the request for a facilitator? Requests can cover a wide range—such as, planning, team-building, clarifying issues, conflict resolution, consultative process and public meeting.

What are the underlying issues?

You may be hired for a team-building session when the underlying issue is a major conflict between a manager and staff over a specific issue or a long-term estrangement between two groups.

What outcomes are required?

What specific outcomes does the client want from the session or workshop? How can these be measured in tangible terms? Are these outcomes achievable?

What other agendas do they have?

If things go exceptionally well, what else will happen? What concerns and fears does the client have? These questions will help to uncover hidden or unclear agendas.

What time is available?

Is the client willing to allocate sufficient time to achieve the desired outcomes? Be careful not to promise to produce results which are not possible in the time allowed. Explain to the client what time is involved and, if sufficient time is not available, lower your promised outcomes to match. How much time processes will take is learned through training and experience. If you are unsure, ask a more experienced facilitator. If the group is new, you may not want to give a provisional estimate until you have met the group and assessed their level of development.

What evaluation is possible?

What feedback mechanisms can be designed both during the facilitation process and after to evaluate to what extent the outcomes have been met? Who will be involved in the evaluation process? Will the evaluation be verbal or written? Who will design the evaluation process? When and where will it take place?

Written confirmation

Confirm the agreements reached in a confirmation letter to the key contact. Include:

The group to be facilitated.

The date, time and venue of sessions to be facilitated. The agreed outcomes and performance measures.

With whom the outcomes were agreed.

The agreed fee or hourly rate and terms of payment (say, within 14 days).

Supplementary services provided (such as printing of notes or research). Evaluation process.

See page 232 for a model letter of confirmation.

Working with an established group

If a group is already established, or will be continuing as an ongoing group, the facilitator works for the whole group. Any agreements negotiated with anyone before meeting the group must be checked out with the whole group to gain their agreement. It is useful if this has been done in writing, with time for anyone to request changes or make objections. In any case, it is a good practice to check your contract at the beginning of the facilitated session, whether or not you have been advised that the group has agreed to it.

It is useful to check the following for agreement:

☐ Your facilitation.

☐ The group outcomes which you have negotiated with someone before the meeting or workshop.

☐ An outline of the process/program that will be followed.

☐ Follow-up.

☐ Evaluation process.

☐ Full participation by group members.

☐ Ground rules.

Your facilitation

After you have introduced yourself and given a short background, ask the group if they are in agreement for you to work with them. Keep the atmosphere light but businesslike:

I have been hired by (name) to facilitate this session/workshop/meeting. Are you all comfortable with my facilitating this session? Does anyone have any problems with this?

Allow time for a response. One or more people will usually say yes and others nod their heads or smile.

If a response is unclear, or people seem to be avoiding eye contact with you, or you sense some underlying tension, check again:

I am unclear about that response. Is everyone okay with my facilitating this session?

If there are objections, write them all up on the board first, then go through them one at a time, responding to the best of your ability. Be honest.

Objections may be on the basis of insufficient experience, being an interested party in proceedings, not being the facilitator preferred by some group members, or associating you with decisions made by another group they don't agree with (a group you are in or have facilitated).

It may be helpful for you to further explain the role of a facilitator, or your own background in response to these concerns. Don't get triggered. Group members' concerns need to be addressed. They don't need to be reasonable or rational.

After you have addressed the concerns as best you can, ask the group:

Are you now able to accept my facilitating this session?

If not, don't continue. It will not work for you or the group, particularly when conflict arises or you are challenged over the process. You need to be clear that you have a contract with the group to work with them.

Checking the outcomes

Next, check out the outcomes you are there to facilitate. It is helpful to have these written down on a whiteboard or large sheets of paper, or have individual copies for each group member.

My understanding is that the group wants the following outcomes from this session. (State the outcomes and measures.)

Then check for agreement (see above). When agreement is given or reached, you have a contract to proceed. If changes are requested, write them up and then negotiate with the whole group for agreement.

Check the proposed process.

I propose to facilitate this by (outline the process/agenda you will use).

Check for agreement and modify if necessary.

Follow-up

It is helpful to clarify at the beginning what follow-up services you will be expected to provide. This may include the printing and distribution of group notes, usually from the whiteboard or large sheets of paper. Check to clarify who will be doing this. If the whiteboard is not electronic, it may be easier to take all notes on paper. The paper sheets can then be taken away and printed out.

Check for evaluation process

Explain the evaluation process briefly and request cooperation with it. It is helpful to allow time for verbal feedback at the end of each session (say 10 minutes), and an opportunity for written evaluation at the end of the series (if a number of sessions are involved).

Check for full participation
If you are facilitating a work group, check to see if participation is voluntary or mandatory. If mandatory, allow participants to express their feelings about that. If there are upsets, suggest that it does not work for people to be present without a choice and invite them to choose to stay or leave. Usually, if participants are given this choice, they will choose to stay. If some participants leave, you will need to check with the group whether it is okay to proceed.

Ground rules
Ask the group if they would like to set some ground rules. These could include confidentiality, punctuality, not leaving the meeting early, commitment to attend all sessions, speaking succinctly, not interrupting, speaking for oneself and not others ("I" statements). You may want to suggest some of these yourself. Remember, ground rules are only useful if they are about things that matter. It is best to start with a few and add to them if needed later. Ground rules need to be displayed prominently so that everyone can see them. Ask the group members to speak up immediately if they see the ground rules being broken.

Public meetings, conferences and other one-time occasions
The situation in these cases is different to that of an ongoing group. Your client will probably be an individual or group of people acting on behalf of a larger organization such as a local government or corporation. Here your contract will be with the

organization (often the local government) responsible for hosting the public meeting or conference. It is essential that you have their agreement to the outcomes and processes to be followed. These may then be stated at the public meeting without debate.

It is important that you, as the facilitator, have the mandate of the key people in the hosting organization to proceed. If you are unsure that the people you are liaising with are the key people, you may like to discuss your concerns with your contact and ask if there is anyone else in the organization who needs to agree to the process.

It is always a good idea to have your contract with a large organization in writing so you have some protection if problems arise at public meetings, as they sometimes do.

Have the most senior key person at a public meeting or conference introduce you and be present throughout the meeting. This is very important as it gives you the stamp of approval and mandate to proceed. If things go wrong, you can then confer with them as to how they want you to proceed. For example, a public meeting may need to be disbanded when protesters or other angry lobby groups become unmanageable. This happened at a meeting where one of the authors was present. Don't make this decision on your own unless you have no alternative. It is better to discuss it with key senior people and recommend what action you think should be taken.

It is best if the person who introduced you closes the meeting.

Handling disruption at a public meeting

Sometimes people come to a public meeting specifically to disrupt it. They could be protesting the subject of the meeting, the host organization, or about some unrelated matter they want to raise in a public forum.

Before a public meeting that is likely to be disrupted, check with the host and agree on a process for handling it. You may decide to:

- Call a short break to allow people to cool down.
- Ignore the disruption.
- Evict disrupters from the meeting.
- Call the police.
- Allow the disrupter to speak with a specified time limit (for example, 5 minutes).
- End the meeting early.

If you intend to evict disrupters, check the legal process for evicting people from a meeting. If problems arise at a public meeting and people need to be asked to leave, it is the role of the key senior person to do this as the host, rather than you as the facilitator. Make sure security people are available to escort the disrupters off the premises.

Facilitating groups of different sizes

As groups increase in size, more structure will be needed and more attention will need to be paid to timing.

Small groups

A group of up to 15 people can work mainly as a whole group, breaking into twos and threes for some sharing and trust-building. A small group provides an opportunity for everyone to speak, and a high level of trust and participation can be developed.

> **Facilitation is creating a space within which people can empower themselves.**

Medium-size groups

Medium-size groups of between 15 and 30 people tend to operate partly as a whole group and partly as a number of formal or informal subgroups. This is a practical solution so everyone can speak and be heard. In-depth creative work, policy development, and report writing are usually carried out by a subgroup, which reports to the larger group for agreement through a nominated spokesperson.

The relationship of subgroups to the larger group needs to be negotiated by the larger group. This negotiation is part of the facilitator's role. Clarity is needed to ensure a subgroup acts within guidelines accepted by the whole group. Time limits, even if informal and self-monitoring, can be helpful to raise participants' awareness.

Listening skills become very important in medium and large groups, and are the main tool for generating synergy. The energy of listening is very potent and calls forth powerful speaking.

Large groups

Large groups (more than 30 people and up to several hundred) require skillful facilitation. Part of the meeting may be held in the large group and part in smaller groups (workshops/task groups). The small groups will usually feed back their discussion and findings to the large group through a spokesperson they have chosen.

The process of a large meeting needs to be planned carefully in advance to ensure the purpose and values are clear, and there is opportunity for maximum participation from those attending. A team of facilitators may be used—the main facilitator working with the large group and assistant facilitators with the subgroups.

The meeting will need to be highly structured, with careful attention given to the time processes will take. For example, if you use a process in which everyone speaks for two minutes in a 60-person group, this will take at least two hours. It will often be necessary to impose time limits on speakers. Structure is more likely to be arbitrary with less opportunity for collective decision-making.

Large groups are useful if an organization wants to transfer information, clarify it by answering questions and get instant feedback. Large groups are less likely to be ongoing. Many people will not have the opportunity to speak in the whole group unless there are strict limits placed on speaking rights—for example, each person can speak only once or twice. Limits may also be needed on the time people can speak. Such structure needs a high degree of cooperation.

Resources such as large electronic whiteboards, overhead projectors, flip charts, newsprint sheets, name tags, masking tape, felt-tipped pens and tables or easels to write on are all useful.

> **Cooperacy, with its collective decision-making, cuts through the formation of group factions.**

Facilitation and Change

In Chapter 1 we explored the philosophy behind facilitation. In this chapter we look at the wider implications of facilitation and cooperative technology, and how they may affect organizations, the community, inter-group conflict, nations and the planet.

Organizational change

Most organizations are continually changing, adapting and transforming, and this is becoming more and more the pattern for survival. The only constant is change, as the saying goes, and it seems to be increasing in velocity. Thus organizational development is focusing more and more on strategic plan-ning, flexible structures, effective communica-tion and clear individual and unit accountabilities.

Organizations are becoming more fluid, less static and rigid. Short-term contracts and self-employment are becoming common as people contract in and out of organizations, or hold part-time contracts with different employers. The value of team-work, consultative processes and participative management are now recognized as integral to workplace reform, and an essential part of business survival and prosperity.

Commitment from individuals to a particular organization has moved from a long-term association and a paternalistic model: *We will look after you and your interests in return for your skills and loyalty* to shorter-term associations and a peer model: *Can we agree on a contract of mutual benefit?* Employees are being required to grow up and negotiate as adults rather than as dependent children.

This adjustment can be very upsetting and painful—like a child being thrust out of the family to fend for itself (laid off) or made to pay an equal share of household expenses after years of being taken care of and paid an allowance (individual contracting and performance management).

This trend towards cooperation between equals and individual responsibility rather than paternalism and dependency creates many difficult areas of adjustment and raises many issues. This is particularly so in relation to collective responsibility and caring for those who are unable to compete equally in the short or long term. These issues will continue to be a focus for concern and debate.

Many organizations are moving toward cooperative processes and cooperative technology in their efforts to survive and adapt. This has created a new accent on cooperative skills, and on acquiring and developing these in organizations. Group-facilitation skills are becoming more and more sought-after, and are a required skill for many management and specialist positions. This is a growing trend.

Facilitators are also setting up businesses in the same way mediators and negotiators have established themselves in recent years.

Democracy is a confrontation-style philosophy which assumes people are on different sides. Its majority decision-making often means win-lose or lose-lose (compromise) outcomes. This leads to frustration and alienation. The increasing rate of change in society requires a different model based on cooperation.

Facilitation Skills

For these reasons, facilitation skills are needed everywhere, but are not yet available in sufficient quantity and quality. More and more people need to aquire these skills so they become everyday currency in all areas of society—in the same way that the democratic model of committee is known by most people and can be applied almost instinctively. Practically everyone knows how to elect a chairperson and secretary, take minutes and make majority decisions—it is part of our culture.

Cooperative technology, such as facilitated meetings and collective decision-making, need to become as much part of our culture conversation as the committee.

Organizations are increasingly able to choose between using in-house or outside facilitators for a range of teamwork, consultative and participatory processes. Training in group-facilitation skills is becoming more available, and the demand will increase.

If there is no facilitation training program available in your area, you can use the Facilitators' Training Program included in this book (pages 169-194). This training program can be implemented by you and a group of from 6 to 12. The program is based on this book and *The Zen of Groups* by the same authors.

We create our own reality.

Consultative processes

Organizations

One of the most effective ways to design and implement organizational change and workplace reform is through vertical-slice consultative bodies. These consultative teams are made up of representatives of all levels and major groupings within an organization, and include the chief executive officer. Union or collective-bargaining representatives are also often included.

The formation of such teams needs to be carefully negotiated, and all key parties need to be consulted. The consultative team is typically between 10 and 20 people, depending on the nature and size of the organization.

The team becomes the development and decision-making body for organizational and cultural change. It is the two-way communication channel between the different parts and levels of the organization. This body does not replace the formal reporting structures of the organization. It becomes an alternative structure with its own framework and rules.

The consultative body usually uses collective decision-making— of necessity. Majority decision-making can polarize the organization and reinforce management-versus-workers thinking or pit one part of the organization against another. This would weaken the value of the consultative body and the process would become counterproductive. The body can therefore correctly be described as a *cooperative body* and it requires the infusion of cooperative skills so it can be effective.

To ensure that neutrality, such bodies often use a facilitator from outside the organization with no internal allegiances. The facilitator takes a key role in guiding the consultative body through the delicate setting-up phase. That's when it develops its purpose, identity, builds trust and commitment, establishes ground rules and boundaries, and builds its vision, goals and objectives.

Sometimes this process will include the development of an organizational charter or code of conduct which then serves as the touchstone for further organizational reform. If a charter is involved, the consultative body will become the communication channel to involve the whole organization in the drafting process. Each consultative member will communicate and hold meetings with staff groups until opportunities for input have been provided for everyone. The processes and ways of working are of crucial importance. The balance between process and task is developed over time, with process being of particular significance.

To ensure that organizational changes are smooth and effective there must be full participation and consultation of all staff. Management will need to trade off power and control for smooth transition and commitment.

Community

Cooperative technology and group facilitation have a longer history in community affairs than in many organizations. Many community groups, particularly those with a personal-development focus, have been using facilitation skills for 10 years or more. Cooperative processes are well established in food and other cooperatives, living communities (owning land and buildings together), in neighborhood networks and grass-roots movements of many kinds (including the women's movement and various protest movements).

Facilitation, rather than the committee model, is now becoming more common at community forums and public meetings. The new-style public meeting hosted by a local authority will use a facilitator rather than a chairperson, with the aim of maximizing public participation and opportunity to speak. This is in contrast to the old-style public debate with a few people dominating, tempers often becoming frayed, and motions and amendments being put and voted on using majority voting.

Government

There is a movement to cooperacy and consensus at the level of national and international governments. The formation of coalitions and the development of more truly representative elective procedures are all paths towards a more consensual and cooperative approach.

The technology of facilitation is the key to effective cooperative government. Facilitators will become common in the corridors of government as cooperative technology is embraced.

Facilitation and mediation

The skills of mediation are better known than those of facilitation. Mediation skills guide the process of two or more opposing parties (individuals or groups) to an agreement. The mediator (unlike an arbitrator) does not make a decision on behalf of the parties. The mediator guides the parties through a process that leads them towards an agreement which they design.

The skills of mediation are allied to those of facilitation in that both are *process guides*. However, the facilitator works within a group and a mediator with opposing parties. A mediator is always involved in conflict of some kind. A facilitator works with conflict within a group, but this is only part of his or her role.

Social change

For humanity and the planet to survive there will need to be a quantum leap in the ability of people and nations to cooperate and find cooperative solutions in an enormous number of areas. We need large-scale access to all aspects of cooperative technology, including facilitation skills. We need to seek out, develop, refine and invent this technology so it is sufficient for the tasks at hand. We need to disseminate this technology throughout the world. These skills are desperately needed at all levels, from the family and households through to governments and the United Nations.

As authors of this book, we are committed to developing and disseminating cooperative technology; and this book, together with our earlier book, *The Zen of Groups,* is part of our commitment to the creation of synergy on the planet.

The value of cooperative skills is that they develop and enhance our ability to cooperate and minimize our tendencies to close ourselves off to others through fear.

The solution and the cure are interconnected. The more we learn how to, the more most of us will want to cooperate.

This book has been written to inspire you to develop your own facilitative skills so you will, in turn, contribute these to your groups and the world.

> **The increasing rate of change in society requires a different model based on cooperation.**

Part 2
Toolkit

Design

A1: Workshop Design

As a facilitator, you will want to have a major input into the design of any workshop you are facilitating. This is process design. Process design is what ensures that the workshop objectives are met and the participants cared for (in the process).

In this section we offer some process-design guidelines and share a workshop model to illustrate how a workshop might look. The workshop length we use in this model is one day, but the guidelines apply to a workshop of any length.

Workshop design guidelines

There are four phases in a workshop. In a one-day workshop, these phases fit broadly into the following four sessions:

Time	Session	Phase
8:30-9:45 am	One	Getting full participation
9:45-10:00 am	Break	
10:00-12:00 pm	Two	Exploring the group limits
12:30-1:00 pm	Lunch break	
1:00-3:00 pm	Three	Claiming new territory
3:00-3:15 pm	Break	
3:15-5:00 pm	Four	Completion

Phases

Each of the four phases has its own intention and flavor. Here is a summary of the contents of each phase. Although not every facet needs to be addressed explicitly (or in exactly this order) in every workshop, the facilitator will be aware of and taking care of them all.

Session One: Getting full participation

The intent of this phase is to have each participant fully present, aligned with the group purpose and ready to work as part of the whole group.

The time needed for this is particularly variable. Time allocated will depend on how well the participants know one another and the clarity of the group purpose. Care taken in this phase is critical as this stage is the foundation on which all other stages rest. This is the phase in which participants are freshest. The facilitator will be establishing credibility and rapport with the group. This phase includes:

Arriving.

Welcoming—may include a ritual.

Handling lateness.

Introduction of the facilitator (including background if a new facilitator). Agreement to the facilitator.

Commitment by participants to be present for the whole session.

Introductions of participants (if one or more new to group).

Statement of group purpose (or objectives of workshop).

Alignment on the purpose.

Housekeeping—including requests.

Clearing session—including any unkept commitments or unfinished business (upsets within or outside the group that will get in the way of everyone being fully present and engaged).

Individual declarations of intention or desired outcomes.

Outline of program—process and content.

Negotiation of and agreement to program.
Setting ground rules if desired, including requests
    for confidentiality.
Clarifying roles.

Session Two: Exploring the group limits

This phase includes:

Clarifying that the group is ready to work.
Exploring the group limits.

The intent of this phase is to explore and develop what the group knows already (or has access to through the facilitator or other resources) so it can move on in the most powerful way. This phase also includes:

Outlining the issues to be addressed.
Establishing the framework for addressing the issues.
Presencing and enlarging the vision or broad picture.
Identifying the resources available to the group.
Receiving specific input.
Deepening the group relationships.
Making connections.
Maintaining focus and concentration.
Pressing the group boundaries.
Identifying where the group's leading edges are (areas it
    can develop).
Clarifying what is missing and how it can be created.
Summarizing where the group is.

Session Three: Claiming new territory

The intent of this phase is for the group to move past the known and claim new territory. This phase includes:

Accessing synergy.
Leaping across chasms.
Breaking through barriers.
Generating creativity.
Maintaining focus.
Sustaining momentum.
Sustaining full participation.
Exploring possibilities.
Developing opportunities.
Maintaining alignment.
Working through conflict.
Clearing baggage.
Sharing withholds.
Keeping energy recharged and moving.
Getting to agreements.

Session Four: Completion

The intent of this phase is to complete the group process in a way that anchors the territory gained by the group. This phase includes:

Completing conversations.
Declaring what has been achieved.
Drawing out the learning.
Presencing the miracles.
Recording decisions.
Recording individual and subgroup commitments.
Creating a structure to support commitments.
Feedback on process and facilitation.

Recognition of territory taken (or lost).

Declarations of individuals' intentions and desired outcomes and whether they were met.

Affirmation of selves and others.

Being ready to leave the group.

Clearing session.

Farewells—may include a ritual.

Workshop model

Here is a workshop model to assist you to translate the design guidelines into a workshop design. The Project Formulation Workshop Model (page 133) will also be useful.

Team-building workshop

This facilitated workshop was designed to increase teamwork in a well-established work group. The promised outcomes were:

1. Development of team skills.
2. Skills in managing conflict.
3. Increased communication skills.

Outcomes were measured by:

1. Feedback from participants at end of workshop.
2. Assessment (to agreed criteria) by manager and staff two weeks later.

Program outline

8:30 am   Welcome, introductions and outline of program for the day. Housekeeping and ground rules.

8:45   Clearing session—what does each participant need to say to be fully present and ready to get to work?

Note: If there is a lot of baggage to be cleared this session can be extended. Move the program times back. Shorten the conflict-management section as needed. You will find you have already covered some of these skills.

9:00	Vision for the team—presented by manager and enlarged by team.
9:15	Trust-building exercise.
9:30	What makes an effective team? Identifying characteristics of an effective team, reaching agreement on checklist, and assessing present team through individual assessment.
10:15	Break.
10:30	Clarification and analysis of power relationships, leadership, roles, and tasks. Sharing strengths and weaknesses through self- and peer assessment. Identifying areas of agreement and differences in perception. Participants choose an area needing improvement and design a plan for working on this.
12:00	Lunch.
12:30 pm	Conflict management, including assertion skills, sharing feelings, and making requests and promises (using role plays).
2:00	Team-building exercise
2:15	Break.
2:30	Developing a team charter and/or contract.
3:45	Identifying the learning.
4:00	Feedback on the day.
4:30	Close.

A2: Meeting Design

Here are the elements of meeting design for a cooperative group using collective decision-making.

Preparation

Checklist:

> Is a meeting necessary? What are the alternatives?
> What is the purpose of the meeting? Is it clear?
> Who needs to be at the meeting? (Key people.)
> Are the key people available?
> Decide date, time and venue.
> Do these arrangements complement the purpose of the meeting?
> Is a written invitation needed? Telephone?
> Does an agenda need to be circulated? Discussed? With whom?
> Do refreshments need to be organized?
> Childcare facilities?
> Transportation Interpreters?
> Is equipment needed? Whiteboard, video, overhead projector, paper, pens. (Generate your own list.)
> Does resource material need to be circulated? Before the meeting?
> Do any key people need to be reminded?
> What results are expected from the meeting?

Environment

Before the meeting, ensure all required resources are prepared and at hand ready to use when appropriate. Prepare the room so it is clean and welcoming, with chairs (and tables, if necessary) set up as you want them for the meeting. Provide only the number of chairs needed.

Arrival

Ensure that people are greeted on arrival and that coats, etc., are attended to. People need time to arrive, greet one another and *get there*, both physically and mentally. The culture of the group (and the organization of which it is a part) is most readily established in the first few minutes of the meeting—even before the meeting proper begins. Think about these questions:

What is the atmosphere you are creating?
Who is responsible for greeting people?
Are people's needs being attended to?
Do people already know one another or are
    introductions needed?

Sit in a circle or round a table without any gaps or empty chairs. Ensure everyone is on the same level—for example, don't have some people on chairs and some on the floor.

Make sure everyone is comfortable—not too hot or cold—and that air is circulating in the room, sufficient light and good sound levels.

Make sure everyone is close enough to hear others clearly and see others' faces. If someone is seated behind another person, request that he come forward and rearrange chairs as required. Repeat the request if necessary.

Ritual

There may be a ritual way of starting your meetings such as a welcome speech or circle.

Establishing roles

Establish who is taking the following roles:

- ☐ Facilitator (responsible for the group process).
- ☐ Recorder (records decisions, agenda items, and people present).
- ☐ Timekeeper (monitors time frames and ending time of meeting).

Introductions

The facilitator checks with the group to see if introductions are needed. Introductions are needed if this is a first meeting or if new people have joined the group.

If appropriate, introduce yourself as facilitator and then invite group members to introduce themselves. This can take the form of a round.

The facilitator checks if everyone is now ready to participate.

Note: People may have personal issues—for example, births, deaths, accomplishments—which they want to share. If a group member is upset or not feeling well, check to see if he or she would prefer not to attend the meeting. Give him or her the opportunity to leave.

Confirm meeting details

The facilitator confirms:

- ☐ Purpose of the meeting and any required outcomes (be specific).
- ☐ Ending time of meeting.
- ☐ Housekeeping details (food arrangements, breaks, location of toilets).

Confirm ground rules (if needed)

Ground rules are optional but useful. They need to be clearly understood and agreed by everyone. Examples of ground rules are:

- ☐ Speaking only for yourself and not on behalf of others.
- ☐ Not interrupting.
- ☐ Speaking succinctly (short and to the point).
- ☐ Not leaving the room until the meeting is completed.
- ☐ Not answering the phone.

Information sharing

Share short items of information which are relevant to the meeting and which do not require discussion (such as apologies for non-attendance). If you find people always get into instant discussion, it may be preferable to put each information item on the agenda.

Review previous decisions

Review all decisions made at the previous meeting and check action taken as a result of decisions.

Record the action taken on each decision. If action has not been taken, record this in the minutes of this meeting. If action is no longer practical or relevant, note this next to the decision in previous records.

Open agenda-setting

This model is often employed by groups using collective decision-making.

Agenda items

Each person puts forward the agenda items he or she wants discussed at the meeting and these are all recorded, preferably on a large sheet of paper so everyone can see. The name of the person who initiated the agenda item is placed beside it.

Time-setting

The initiator is asked by the facilitator to estimate how long it will take to discuss the item and the requested time is noted beside the item. The facilitator checks this time with the group and adjusts if a longer time is requested.

Priority-setting

The times of all items are added together and the ending time of the meeting checked. If the time needed is longer than the time of the meeting, have a round where each person nominates two most important agenda items. These can be recorded next to the item by marking one check for each person's preferences. This will generate a priority list and items can be addressed in this order. Keep in mind the following:

What items must be discussed today?
What items are important but not urgent?
What items can be left until another meeting or be resolved by another process—for example, delegation to one or two people to decide and act upon?

Discussion, decision-making and action-planning

Each agenda item is now discussed in turn. The following process may be useful.

1. The facilitator invites the initiator to:

☐ Introduce the item (issue and background).
☐ Say what he or she wants from the group (feedback, ideas, alternatives or a decision).
☐ Suggest the process or technique he or she would like the group to use—for example, rounds, brainstorm, pros and cons.

2. The facilitator seeks clarification and group agreement that the ideas outlined by the initiator should be implemented. If the initiator is unclear about techniques or processes, the facilitator will suggest one. If specific feedback or ideas are requested, the facilitator may find the technique of rounds useful. Often a round will clarify the issue, and common ground and differences will become obvious.

3. When this process is complete, the facilitator summarizes and checks to see what else is needed for the initiator's request to be fulfilled.

4. If group agreement is needed, request proposals from the group. Continue this process until a proposal is suggested which meets general agreement. It may be helpful to reach minor agreements along the way. Record these. If a decision is being held up by one or two people, the facilitator can ask what they propose to solve the difficulty. If agreement is still not reached, check with dissenters to see if they are directly affected by the outcome. If not, see if they will allow the decision to be made anyway.

    Those directly affected by a decision need to be directly involved in the decision-making.

5. The timekeeper keeps an eye on the time and lets the meeting know how it is going. It is usually better not to extend time, as there is a group "law" that decision-making expands to fill the time available. Not extending time educates the group to be intentional in decision-making.

6. If a decision is not made, you may need an interim decision such as:
- ☐ Deferring the item to next or a special meeting.
- ☐ Delegating one or more people to decide on behalf of the group within given parameters.

Records

Records of the meeting need to include:

People present.
Date and time.
Agenda items.
Decisions made.

Write down each decision as it is reached, including specific actions, if any, to be taken. Note who will take action on the decision and by when. Always be very specific.

Next meeting

Decide the date and time of the next meeting.

Completion

A closing round may be held in which people express anything that is still incomplete for them from the meeting, or any feedback they would like to give to other members of the group.

Ending

The group may have a ritual for ending the group.

Follow-up

After the meeting, circulate decisions to participants. Alternatively, you may keep a decision book in a central place.

A useful tool between meetings is to set up a decision-management system. This could take the form of buddies who coach each other toward taking the action they said they would by the time promised. Another method is to nominate a decision manager who keeps in contact with people carrying out decisions and coaches them to meet their commitments.

House-meeting model

This meeting model is designed for regular weekly household meetings of 45 minutes maximum. Have a facilitator, recorder and timekeeper. Rotate these roles. Write decisions in a book and keep in a public place. *(Note:* This model can easily be modified for a work-group meeting.)

9:00 am	Cup of coffee (prepared by timekeeper, who also calls people to the meeting).
	Information sharing.
9:10	Review of previous decisions. Indicate in book whether completed, carried forward or deleted.
9:15	Set open agenda with times (write in book).
9:20	Discussion, decision-making and action-planning.
	Record decisions in book.
9:45	End of meeting with some kind of ritual.
	(Dale's house meetings end with a group hug.)

(See page 235 for a model of a meeting record sheet.)

A3: Project Design

An effective group will have a clear purpose and vision, and undertake projects to help achieve its purpose. It is very helpful for a facilitator to understand the basics of project design so that the easiest path for achieving the project can be found.

Examples of projects

Projects are specific desired results in a given time. They can involve one or more people. Three examples are:

- [ ] To increase the school enrollment by 10 percent by March 1.
- [ ] To complete the construction of . . . building to . . . standard by . . . time.
- [ ] To hold a birthday party on May 24 at . . . with . . . people present.

Project stages

There are four stages in any project—formulation, concentration, momentum and completion. Here is a summary of each stage and the kind of issues that are likely to arise.

Formulation

This is the first stage of a project. In this stage, the nature of the project is developed and clarified from the initial good idea to a specific and measurable objective. The project is checked for its importance in realizing the vision, its priority in relation to other projects, its feasibility and the commitment and resources of the group for carrying it out.

Ask the group these questions:

Does the project move the group toward its vision?

Is this project the best use of group time, effort and resources?
Is the project attainable?
Is the project a sufficient challenge?
Can every single person own the project and be committed to it?
What are people's concerns about the project? (Get them all out in the open.)
Is it exciting, does it light up or inspire group members?
Are all the group members aligned on the project?

The project needs to be written in terms of a SMART objective—

Specific
Measurable
Attainable
Results-orientated
Time bound

Sometimes there will be more than one objective.

The project must have specific conditions of satisfaction or performance measures. The objective will need an action plan with sufficient detail to show that the project can be fulfilled. A fully formulated project will leave no doubt as to its feasibility— and this does not mean that it won't stretch every member of the team to get it done.

Alarm bells

☐ The project is unclear or unmeasurable.
☐ The project is not central to fulfilling the vision.
☐ Some group members are not excited or have become quiet.

Do not proceed until the project is clear and measurable, it has been modified to meet the vision, and the group members are fully aligned and excited. Any question marks now mean danger later.

Concentration

In the concentration stage of the project, the group will be putting in a lot of energy fine-tuning and implementing the action plan. This is the high-energy action stage when coordinate action is required among all team members. It is time to get the wheel in motion and it takes more energy to get the wheel started than to keep it in motion. It is high energy in for small results out.

Ask the group these questions:

Are the action plans clear and comprehensive?
Has a project manager been appointed to manage the action-plan implementation?
Is everyone clear what actions he or she is accountable for?
Are the time frames clear?
Is there feedback—early-warning systems in place for problems?
Is there a clear display of the project (such as a wall chart) where everyone can see at a glance what is happening?
Are there any problems with getting access to resources?
Is anyone stuck, confused and needing help?
Does anyone need coaching to carry through with his or her tasks?
Has anyone bitten off more than he or she can chew?
Are there clear communication channels or lines?
Is everyone in communication or are some people stuck and withholding their problems?
Are there clear problem-solving and conflict-resolution mechanisms?

Alarm bells

☐ People are out of communication with one another—not returning phone calls, not checking in as arranged or not using the feedback systems. This is nearly always the first indication that something is wrong.

- [ ] People look hassled and avoid eye contact.
- [ ] Time frames are starting to slip.
- [ ] The wall display (or other display) is not up to date.
- [ ] People are withholding their problems.

Encourage the group to take action at the first signs of problems—and there will always be some. Get people back into communication, sharing problems, recreating the vision and clarifying commitments. Trust that the group can solve any problems that arise. Celebrate small victories. Act on the assumption that problems not shared always get worse. Without rigorous management the project may never get to the next stage.

Momentum

If the concentration stage has been effective, the project will now move into momentum. This is the stage when the wheel is turning and needs to be steered rather than pushed. Less energy is needed to drive the project and results are showing up. The project is on course (or close to it) and the wall display will reflect the good results. It is clear that the project will be successful (in whole or part). People can take some time out to reflect on progress and acknowledge the efforts and successes of one another.

Ask the group these questions:

Is management in place—who is steering the project and watching out for danger?
Is the wall display up to date?
Is the momentum being maintained?
Who is out of communication and why?
Do the action plans need updating?
Is it time to have a clearing session?

What is missing that could make a difference in completing the project?

Alarm bells

- ☐ People are losing focus and concentration.
- ☐ People seem to be satisfied with less than full, successful completion of the project.
- ☐ The project manager is not being vigilant in steering the project—it is getting off course.

Focus and concentration need to be maintained to ensure that the project remains on course, and that everyone is available for extra energy to solve any further problems which arise. Vigilance and watchfulness are the keys to keep the momentum going. Remember accidents at speed are much more dangerous than when you are traveling slowly.

Completion

This is the last stage of the project, when the final results are collated and all the loose ends are tied up. Evaluations are carried out. All the learning from this project is distilled so that further projects can benefit. Any leftover gripes and disappointments are shared. Acknowledgments to one another and others are given and successes celebrated. A completion ritual is carried out. People are free to begin the next project.

Ask the group these questions:

Have the project outcomes been achieved?
Is the display complete?
Is anything missing which can still be put in?
Have all the action plans been completed or revoked?

Has all the learning from the project been spoken and written?
Has a completion meeting been held to express any unfinished
    business with one another?
Have full acknowledgments occurred?
Is everyone complete and freed up to move to the next project?
Has there been full celebration?

This stage is often glossed over and the full learning is not accessed. Encourage people to say everything they need to say—to withhold nothing, whether it appears large or small. A small issue on this project may be critical on the next. Make sure people get the opportunity to acknowledge themselves and one another fully. This is the real reward everyone wants and needs—where our cup gets refilled.

Alarm bells

☐ People look hassled—they are not freed up and complete.
☐ The learning is superficial.
☐ The fullness of acknowledgment is missing.
☐ There is no clear ending ritual.

Project-formulation workshop model

This model is of a day workshop for a project group of up to 25 people and a facilitator. The purpose of the workshop is to formulate (clarify and develop) the project and get it off to a strong start. The model is suitable for an organization project or a community project.

The promised outcomes are:

1. Clear project objectives and action plans.
2. Commitment to fulfill the project.

Outcomes are to be measured by:

1. Written objectives and action plans with time limits.
2. Clear accountabilities.
3. Ongoing meeting structure in place for project group.

Program outline

9:30 am   Welcome by senior staff member (or community leader for community project) and introduction of the facilitator.

You, as facilitator, give some background to establish credibility and explain how you will work with the group (whole group and subgroups).

Outline of program for the day. Check for agreement to proceed. Negotiate if there are requests for changes.

Housekeeping (food, toilets, ending and break times).

9:50   Introductions. An exercise or process for participants to meet each other and establish some rapport. See *The Zen of Groups* Toolkit for ideas on how to do this.

10:15   The project idea is introduced to the group by the initiators. Although all participants will already know about the project and be interested in being involved, they will not have heard it as a group.

10:30   Morning break.

10:45   Building the vision of the project, as a round or brainstorm. Involve all of the participants so they contribute to the building of the project and own it. Record key words of all comments on sheets of paper.

11:30	Developing goals and objectives. Crystallizing the vision in specifics. Use subgroups to work on these, with five people in each group. Groups report back to the whole group after 20 minutes.
	Then, working with the whole group, refine, prioritize and negotiate agreement. Ensure that objectives are specific, measurable and time-bound.
12:30 pm	Break for lunch.
1:15	Strategies, resources—brainstorm strategies and resources needed to meet each objective. List on large sheets of paper.
	List where the resources can come from. Use subgroups, one for each objective, for 30 minutes. Then allow 10 minutes for participants to move to other groups to add to the lists.
	Pin sheets up around the room.
2:30	Accountabilities—request participants to break up into task teams, one for each objective. In the task teams, have each team member share what time and other resources he or she can contribute or access. Each team records this and chooses a team leader before developing an action plan and allocating specific tasks to each team member.
3:15	Break for tea or coffee.
3:30	Each task team shares with the whole group what they will be doing. Actions may need to be coordinated in the large group.

3:50	Ongoing structure developed—coordinating group or task team groups or other agreed structure. Further meetings arranged.
4:30	Feedback on day.
4:45	Closing address by senior staff member or community leader.

A4: Evaluation Design

What is the purpose of evaluation?

The purpose of evaluation is to determine the value or worth of something. The questions underlining evaluation are:

What did we plan to achieve?
Did we achieve it?
To what standard did we achieve it?
What have we learned that can be applied in the future?

The design of evaluation

The design of evaluation is part of planning. At the planning phase of a workshop, project or other process, we design how it will be evaluated. And having implemented the workshop, project or process, we then evaluate it as agreed during the planning phase.

Smart and soft evaluation

Smart evaluation is evaluation against measurable outcomes—for example, the achievement of a SMART objective (Specific, Measurable, Attainable, Results-oriented and Time-bound).

Soft evaluation is evaluation which is expressive and descriptive—of individuals' feelings, perceptions, learnings and insights.

SMART objectives set in the planning stage allow for clear monitoring during the project and evaluation at the end. Lack of measurable outcomes mean that evaluation can only be soft.

Large quantities of soft evaluation do not compensate for lack of planning with measurable outcomes, such as SMART objectives.

Make sure that each project has identified the key measurable outcomes that will show whether or not the project has been accomplished. These need to be displayed, tracked and made available to be seen by all participants. See A3: Project Design.

We recommend a mix of smart and soft evaluation—and measurable outcomes for the overall process, workshops and meetings plus expressive and descriptive spoken and written material from individual participants.

Smart evaluation

Smart evaluation is straightforward. Clear outcomes and measures are developed in the planning stage and these are then applied in the evaluation stage. The clearer and more specific the stated outcomes, the simpler the evaluation process. Clear evaluation requires a SMART approach. These outcomes or objectives can then be measured by numbers, percentages or yes/no responses.

Smart evaluation model

1. Were the promised outcomes met?
   Outcome A: Yes/No or percent or fraction.
   Outcome B: Yes /No or percent or fraction.
   Outcome C: Yes/No or percent or fraction.
   Total number of outcomes met:

2. Outcome A: The process was implemented as agreed.
(Yes/No)
Outcome B: The strategic plan (content) completed.
(Yes/No)
Outcome C: All time frames were met. (Yes/No)

Soft evaluation

Soft evaluation is useful where the outcomes are qualitative—about quality rather than quantity—or unpredictable. Soft evaluation provides expression for learning that is not directly related to the stated outcomes. It allows for lateral thinking and unexpected results. It can also provide an opening for a new and different future.

Soft evaluation is usually in response to open questions—questions which cannot be answered by yes or no:

What was useful?
What was not useful?
What did you learn?
How did you feel?
What insights did you have about yourself or others? What are your
recommendations for the future?

Responses are likely to be expressive and descriptive:

I realized that I am an excellent team leader. I have gained a lot of
confidence.
I got a real shock to see how my behavior affected the team results.
I was amazed that . . . happened. I would never have predicted it.

Soft evaluation models

1. Feedback by participants at the end of each facilitated session. Two structured or unstructured rounds:
   (a) Constructive criticism.
   (b) Acknowledgments.
   Comments can be recorded on a large sheet of paper.

2. Half-way evaluation by participants for a series of facilitated sessions. Participants complete the following sentences either as a round or in writing:
   What I have gained from the content so far is . . .
   What I still want to accomplish is . . .
   What I appreciate about the process is . . .
   My suggestions for improvement are . . .

3. Evaluation by participants at the end of a series of facilitated sessions. Participants complete the following sentences either as a round or in writing:
   What I have accomplished as a result of these sessions is . . .
   The action I will take as a result of these sessions is . . .
   What was missing from these sessions was . . .
   The improvements to the content I recommend are . . .
   The improvements to the process I recommend are . . .

Softly smart

A mixed evaluation for individual participants at a training workshop can involve each individual setting his or her own specific learning objectives at the beginning of the workshop and reviewing these at the end.

B # Facilitative Processes

The following processes are for training the facilitator. The focus is on peers or the peer group, where the aim is for everyone to become self-, other- and group-facilitative. As such, these processes are a powerful adjunct to the Facilitators' Training Program, page 169. These processes are also useful for a facilitator to use in groups they are facilitating.

The Zen of Groups includes a Toolkit of 95 techniques and exercises to assist any group to become more effective and synergistic. Many of these techniques (rounds, brainstorms, subgroups, pros and cons, continuums) are the basic tools for any facilitator. If you are unsure about any basic techniques, we recommend that book.

Read each of these processes carefully before using them so you understand them fully.

With a group, it may be helpful to read the process aloud. Otherwise, begin by describing the process to the group and seeking their agreement to use it. If there is opposition, provide an opportunity for people to express it, and listen for natural apprehension about new ways of doing things. After concerns have been expressed, respond to them and encourage the group to feel the fear and do it anyway.

However, don't force the group to do a process against its will— the process won't work without agreement. Processes work best if everyone has fun with them and they are done with a light touch.

B1 Being with Another

Purpose: To experience being fully present to yourself and another person.

Time: 5 minutes, increasing to 40 minutes over time.

Process: In pairs, sit facing one another and establish eye contact. Bring all your available attention to being with the other person. Notice your thoughts, feelings and body sensations without attachment to them. Note them and let them go. At the end of the agreed time, share your experience with one another.

Variations:

☐ Do this exercise by yourself, looking in a mirror.

☐ Do this exercise with other forms of life such as trees, stones and the sea.

B2 Being with a Group

Purpose: To experience being fully present to yourself and other members of the group.

Time: 5 minutes.

Process: Stand or sit in a circle, facing one another. Become aware of your breathing. Do not cross your arms or legs.

Center your attention in your belly and imagine you are like a tree with a root system deep within the ground and branches reaching toward the sky. Be aware of your physical body, your energy and the space around you.

Now allow yourself also to become aware of the other group members. Focus your attention on each group member in turn. Observe each one's physical body, energy and relationship to the space around them. Move your attention around the group. Focus on each group member in turn for a short period (say 10 seconds). Do not seek out or avoid eye contact. Do not linger long with any one person.

Keep your attention moving so that you become present to everyone in the group. Continue to pay attention to your breathing. Keep it relaxed and deep. Become aware of the group as a whole. Be with the group and each person in it. Include yourself in this. Bring the purpose and the vision of the group to mind. Allow any feelings and thoughts to come and go. Focus on being with the group.

The exercise will end naturally or can be ended by the facilitator, who will thank the group.

Variations:

- [ ] Do this exercise while holding hands, left hand palm up, right hand palm down. Be present to the energy in the group and between your hands.
- [ ] Do this exercise while standing with arms around each other's shoulders.
- [ ] Immediately after this exercise, while in the same positions, chant or sing together.
- [ ] Do this exercise with your eyes closed. Imagine or sense each person rather than looking at them.
- [ ] This exercise can also be done by any individual group member at any time.

B3 My World, Your World

Purpose: To illustrate our different worlds through a visual display (for two or more people).

Materials: A large sheet of paper (such as newsprint) for each person and an assortment of colored pens.

Time: 1 hour.

Process: Each participant chooses six of the following categories that most interest him or her. Suggestions for categories: Work, home, relationships, physical, emotional, mental, spiritual, play, recreation, the world, the universe, making a difference, other beings, garden, environment, creativity, wellbeing, training and development, politics. You may like to work in different rooms.

Individually and without conversation divide your piece of paper into sections, one for each category you have chosen. In each section on the sheet, write the name of the category and then your responses to the questions listed below. You may like to use particular colors, shapes, symbols or words which have meaning for you.

What are the most important things to me in this category?
What are my hopes and fears?
What do I want more of? Less of?
What are my areas of development?
What is one action I intend to take in the next week?

Work/play through each category in turn. After you have completed all the categories you may want to mark some connections between them or other insights.

Come back together when you are finished or at a prearranged time (say, after 30 minutes) and share your worlds one at a time.

Go into detail. Allow others to ask for clarification of your picture. Avoid assessment and judgment about another's world. Accept it as a display of who each person is.

When this process is completed, compare your pictures for differences and similarities. If done as a group exercise, you may want to pin them up on a wall. Share your perceptions and insights.

Thank one another for revealing your worlds.

B4 Mining the Gold

Purpose: To develop listening skills so as to discover the *gold* in another's speaking.

Materials: None.

Time: 45 minutes.

8 minutes for each focus—(4 minutes x 2 people). 3 minutes introduction and 10 minutes sharing in whole group at end of exercise. The facilitator will act as timekeeper.

Process: Working in pairs choose an A and a B. A is the listener and B the speaker. B speaks for two minutes on any topic while A listens for the concerns of B (spoken or in the background). For one minute A reflects back to B the concerns he or she heard. B listens for recognition of really being heard. One minute is then spent in sharing and coaching:

Yes, you got my concerns.
Yes that rang true.
You recognized concerns that were unspoken or that I was unclear about.
I felt really heard.
You didn't hear my concerns.
I didn't feel listened to.
You put in some concerns that don't ring true (maybe your own).

Swap roles and repeat.

Repeat the exercise for each of the three remaining listening focuses.

The four listening focuses are:

1. Concerns of the speaker.
2. Commitments of the speaker.
3. Contribution of the speaker.
4. Magnificence of the speaker.

Possible topics for speaker:
Any topic of interest to the speaker will work equally well. If speakers are stuck for a topic, encourage them to choose one for which they have energy. Give examples such as:

Work project.
Family.
Relationship.
Hobby.
Starting the day.
Favorite weekend activities.
Work problems.
Political issue.

Complete exercise with sharing in the whole group. Ask:

How was that exercise?
Did you experience being recognized or really heard? What was this like?
How do you feel about it?

Variations:

☐ Change partners for each listening focus.
☐ Change the listening focus when pairs swap roles. This will halve the time of the exercise.

B5 Speaking the Vision

Purpose: A coaching exercise to develop powerful speaking. This is an inspiring process and a good one to have right before a break or at the end of a session.

Time: 40 minutes total (for 10 people).

5 minutes introduction, including short demonstration.

10 minutes for coaching in pairs (5 minutes x 2).

20 minutes (2 minutes each) in the whole group.

5 minutes debrief.

Process: In pairs, A speaks his or her vision on a theme of his or her choice. B listens and coaches A in two areas:

1. To remove all limiting or qualifying words. For example:

I would like to see.
Fairly important.
I suppose that . . .
I might be able to do it . . .
It would be great if . . .
I would love that but . . .
If only . . .

The coaching needs to be direct—for example, "Say that again without the *but*."

2. To enlarge the picture and speak expressively. For example:

Can you say that more expansively?

Can you show your enthusiasm with your face and tone of voice?
Can you describe that more fully?
Can you say that in a way that lights you up?

Swap roles and repeat.

Come back to whole group. Each person now speaks his or her vision expressively and without qualification, uninterrupted, to the whole group.

Suggestions for vision focus:

My ideal living environment.
World peace.
Healing the planet.
The perfect team to be part of.
My children's future.
My brilliant career.
My work for the world.

Variations:

☐ Work in twos but allow 8 to 10 minutes for each person.
☐ Work in threes with a coach and a listener, for 5 minutes each.
☐ In the whole group, the facilitator coaches participants until the vision is powerful.

B6 Empowering Interpretations

Purpose: To invent an empowering interpretation of a
problem or conflict. This exercise builds on the skills
developed in the two previous processes.

Time: 35 minutes.

10 minutes x 2 people, plus 5 minutes introduction
and 10 minutes sharing in whole group.

Process: In pairs, A speaks about a problem, area of concern or
conflict he or she is currently involved with (3 minutes). B listens
for the concerns, commitment, contribution and vision of the
speaker. B then feeds back what he or she heard through his or
her powerful listening (3 minutes). A now invents a new and
empowering interpretation of the problem, building on the feedback from the listener. B can also add coaching at this point
(3 minutes). The pair finishes by debriefing (1 minute).

Swap roles and repeat.
Bring the whole group back together and invite one or two
people to share their new interpretations.

Variation:

☐ As part of the introduction the facilitator works with a
participant in front of the group to demonstrate the process.
Allow an additional 5 minutes.

B7 Identity Check (for Uncovering Projections)

Purpose: An identity check uncovers the projections we are making onto others. We all do this with everyone we meet. This exercise is particularly useful if you are beginning a close working or personal relationship or if a relationship is becoming difficult or stuck.

Time: Variable—say 20 minutes (10 minutes x 2).

Process: Sit opposite each other on the same level and maintain eye contact. Person A asks B the following questions, encouraging B to answer them as fully as possible:

> *Who do I remind you of?*
>
> *How am I like him?*
>
> *What do you want to say to him? Say it to me now as if I were that person.*
>
> *What do you want him to say to you? (A then repeats this back to B as though that person were speaking.)*
>
> *How am I different from that person? (Continue asking this question until both of you are clear that you are quite distinct from that person.)*

You may find that a person reminds you of more than one other and the whole process will need to be repeated.

When B has completed the process, swap roles and begin again.

B8 Situation Check (for Uncovering Projections)

Purpose: A situation check uncovers the projections we are making from one situation onto others. This exercise is particularly useful if you find you are reacting to a situation out of proportion to its significance or if feelings about a situation are hanging around after the event.

Time: Variable—say 10 minutes.

Process: Ask yourself or have someone else ask you the following questions:

What does this situation remind me/you of?
How is it similar?
What do I/you need to express to get complete about the other situation?
    (Feelings, thoughts, unexpressed communications or sounds.)
What would I/you like to have happened differently?
Whom do I/you need to forgive? (Including my/yourself)?
How is this situation different from the previous one? (Describe
    differences in detail until both of you are clear that this situation
    is quite distinct from the previous situation.)

You may find that the situation reminds you of more than one other situation and the whole process will need to be repeated.

Variation:

☐ This exercise can also be reciprocal. After the exercise is completed, swap roles and repeat.

B9 Role Plays

Purpose: To try out different behavior in a safe environment where assistance and feedback are available.

Process: Suggest a role play when a situation occurs where a different behavior may be useful.

1. Ask the person (key player):

   Would you like to try out some different ways of responding in that situation? Are you willing to do a role play?
   If willing to proceed, invite the person to move to a new place (say, in front of the group). Sit/stand beside him or her.

2. Check the purpose of the person doing the role play.

   What do you want to accomplish out of this role play?

3. After the primary player has answered that question, have him or her briefly describe the situation and the people who are part of it. Allow no more than two minutes for this.

4. The primary player then chooses people to take the other roles, and where they will sit or stand. The other players move to their positions and model the part as described by the primary player.

   Sit the way that person sits and say what that person says.

5. After this briefing, the primary player returns to his or her role-play position and chooses who starts and exactly what they say. The other players respond within the roles described.

6. If the primary player gets stuck, the facilitator can:

☐ Invite coaching suggestions from the group.
☐ Invite the primary player to swap roles with another player.
☐ Invite the primary player to swap places with a member of the group not involved in the role play and observe the situation being acted out.
☐ Invite the primary player to take on a coach from the observers and have the coach stand/sit beside him or her and make suggestions.

7. The primary player practices one or more different ways of handling the situation until finding the one that feels right.

8. If the primary player agrees, invite feedback from the group on the new behvior.

9. Deroling:
Debrief from the roles.

"I am not like . . . I am . . . and I . . . (outline differences).
All players must derole themselves and the other players. Make sure they are back in their own selves before you continue. If unsure, get them to add up numbers in their heads until they are deroled. If the key player cannot hug the other players at the end of the exercise, he or she is not deroled.

Variation:

☐ Use cushions as alternatives to people for roles. Remember to have the key player derole the cushions after the exercise. If the key player rejects the cushion after the exercise or wants it removed, he or she is not deroled. (We have had people want cushions destroyed or never brought back to a group.)

B10 Uncovering Sabotage Patterns

Purpose: To identify and share the ways in which each participant's patterned behavior is likely to get in the way
of the group achieving its purpose.

Note: This is a consciousness-raising exercise, not an
excuse for blaming others or oneself. The mood
needs to be lightly serious.

Time: 30 to 60 minutes, depending on size of group.

Process: In pairs, choose an A and a B.
1. For 3 minutes, A asks B:

How do you sabotage yourself?
A encourages B to be specific and invites him or her to think
of other ways:
Yes, and how else do you sabotage yourself?
Swap roles for 3 minutes.

2. For 3 minutes, A asks B:

How do you sabotage others?
A encourages B to be specific and think of other ways he
or she sabotages others.
Swap roles for 3 minutes.

3. In the whole group, ask members to share as an unstructured
round, giving each person 2 to 3 minutes:

How do you sabotage a group?
Members may like to ask the group for suggestions.

4. In pairs, design an alarm system for each person's sabotage
pattern (5 minutes total).

5. Invite members to share their alarm systems in the whole group or ask for suggestions (optional).

6. Debrief from this exercise as a whole group with a group hug or scream.

B11 Clearing Processes

Clearing processes are about letting go of blocks, withheld communications and patterned behavior, which get in the way of our being fully present both to ourselves and to others. Clearing processes provide a space for rich authentic relating, and the presencing of love and cooperation. They require commitment and the courage to break through our comfort zone and our own ideas about ourselves and others. They seem scary, take time and can't be hurried, although facilitation can assist to quicken the pace.

Indications for a clearing session

Indications that a clearing session is needed could be one or more of the following:

- ☐ A vague feeling of discomfort with an individual or the group.
- ☐ A reluctance to participate fully in the relationship or the group.
- ☐ Avoiding eye contact with someone or a number of people.
- ☐ Not having much fun together.
- ☐ Low energy.
- ☐ Often feeling irritable with someone or a number of people.

- [ ] A certainty that you are right about something and someone else is wrong.
- [ ] A feeling of resignation or hopelessness about your relationship with someone or the group.
- [ ] A feeling of alienation from others.
- [ ] Yawning not related to lack of sleep.
- [ ] Inability to reach agreement on specific issues.

Clearing processes are always voluntary. Most people have little or no experience of being clear with other people, and react to each other out of old patterns and unfinished business—usually from their parents and families of origin. So these processes are revolutionary and, if used regularly, would totally alter the way we relate to one another. The main thing to watch for is people projecting distress onto others (making it their fault) and stopping the process before all all clearing has been completed.

B11a One-to-One Clearing

One of the participants invites another to have a clearing session.

> *I'm feeling uncomfortable around you. I'm not sure exactly what*
> *it's about. Can we meet to have a clearing session? Are you*
> *available now?*

If the other person is willing but unavailable at that time, arrange
a time and place. You may want to negotiate to have a facilitator
present or agree to call on one if you get stuck.

Start the session by each declaring what you are committed to
in the relationship, yourself and the other person. For example:

> *I am committed to our friendship (or good working relationship) and*
> *want to be relaxed around you. And I want you to be comfortable*
> *around me, too.*

Then describe the feeling or behavior which you have noticed in
yourself. Seek to identify the incident. There always is one.

> *I noticed that I was uncomfortable (or annoyed) when . . . happened.*
> *Having said that, what I now see is that . . .*
> *And what's underneath that is . . .*
> *And the feelings I have about that are . . .*

The hard things to say are usually feelings which we don't like
to experience in ourselves or admit to others. They often seem
petty and despicable—such as jealousy, anger and unwillingness
to lend or share things, or feelings of being invaded or taken
advantage of or of being subjected to too many demands. The
feelings often don't fit with our own image of ourselves as being
generous and tolerant. They often seem to relate more to our
childhood than to the present.

Own all the feelings as your own and tell the other person what behavior triggered them without judgment of right or wrong, good or bad, of either yourself or the other person. This is often the hardest part.

You may also be reminded of past incidents with that person or someone else where something similar happened. Say this too.

Another situation I remember is . . .
And when that happened I felt . . .

Keep speaking, without interruption, until you can go no further, and then the other person has a turn to do the same.

There may be requests and promises you both want to make along the way or at the end.

I request that when that situation happens again you . . .
    (be specific).

When the other person has finished, have further turns until you each are fully clear.

If you get stuck or it is too scary to continue, either person may call time out and renegotiate to meet again with a facilitator. Relationships, particularly close working and personal ones, will bring up all our old unhealed patterns from the past, many to do with our parents and siblings. You almost certainly will have touched on deep hurts and primal feelings. Personal therapeutic work may be needed.

Indications that clearing is complete
You will know when you are fully clear because you will feel empty but complete. There is nothing left to say. You are freed up to be with yourself and the other person. You have the space to appreciate, recognize and love them.

When the process is complete, thank one another and acknowledge the courage and magnificence shown by both of you.

Variation:

☐ After each turn, the listener reflects back the essence of what was said as a checking process. The speaker needs to be satisfied with the reflection before the other person has a turn.

Use this variation for all or part of the time. It is most useful when one or both people are becoming very triggered. When we are triggered, we tend to remember only the trigger phrase and not the other things said.

B11b Group Clearing

This is similar to one-to-one clearing and can involve some or all members of the group. The indications that a clearing session is needed are the same as for one-to-one clearing and are listed there. If only two participants or a small section of a group are involved, the clearing session may be best done outside group time. Use the one-to-one clearing process and adapt it to two or more people.

If most of the group are involved, you may choose to have a clearing session (preferably right away) or schedule a special group clearing session if it appears likely that a longer time is needed. Read One-to-One Clearing, pages 158 to 160, as a preparation for this process.)

Note: If the group is a cooperative group, you will usually have a commitment to reach agreement. If the group is a hierarchical or ad hoc group, you will now need to consider whether you are prepared to make a commitment to get clear and reach agreement. This will include determining if there is sufficient safety (confidentiality and power balance) for people to allow themselves to be vulnerable. This process is not appropriate for uncommitted groups.

Purpose: To bring the group back to its purpose and vision, and clear any baggage which is getting in the way of the group being turned on and energized.

Time: Variable—could be anywhere from 30 minutes to 3 hours. There needs to be a commitment to see the process through.

Materials: Whiteboard

Process: Declare a breakdown in the group

Stop. This is not working. Let's have a clearing session.
Check for agreement to continue with the clearing process. If there is agreement, continue as follows. Have someone speak the purpose and the vision of the group.

Our purpose is . . . Our vision is . . .

If the purpose and vision are unclear, this may be the issue.

Then invite participants to identify what is getting in the way of their full participation in the group.

What is getting in the way for me is . . .

Take turns in uninterrupted rounds. Listen generously to one another. Continue with the rounds until the group is clear.

Encourage group members to own their own feelings and thoughts rather than project them onto others. If requests are made in the rounds, write them on a whiteboard to be addressed after the rounds are completed.

When the rounds have been completed (see Indications that clearing is complete, page 159), ask for any further specific requests and add these to the whiteboard. Address requests one at a time. Have members accept, or decline and counteroffer. If no counteroffer is acceptable, ask the whole group to suggest solutions.

If the group cannot come to agreement, an indication that the group is still not clear, do Being with Another, Process B1, or Being with a Group, Process B2, before going any further. Then, go back to the beginning of this exercise and repeat the process.

Do not finish the session until the group is complete. If you have repeated the exercise three times and the group is still not clear, ask each person to choose whether or not to remain in and recommit to the group. Provide an opportunity for people to leave the group without a feeling of failure.

When the process is complete, thank and acknowledge one another for your and their courage and magnificence.

Variation:

☐ As for One-to-One Clearing, Process B11a.

B11c Clearing Yourself when Facilitating

Tell the group you are triggered and call a short break. Then:

Take an uninvolved group member aside and ask him or her to ask you:

What do you need to say or do to get clear?

You will probably be feeling angry and need to express this in some way. You may prefer to do this in another room, out of earshot, by jumping up and down or screaming. If you are concerned about noise, you can scream into a towel

If it's inappropriate to use a group member, ask yourself the same question and take similar action.

B12 Getting Fully Present

Purpose: To enable participants to get themselves fully present and engaged in the group, and to build group consciousness. A good process to use at the start of any small group meeting. (For larger groups see Variation.)

Time: Will vary depending on the number of people, the purpose of the group, the balance of process and task, individual awareness levels and the degree of commitment to group consciousness.

For task-focused groups 1 to 2 minutes per person may be sufficient.

For in-depth development and creative groups, this process will take however long is needed and may include in-depth clearing in the group. (See Clearing Processes, Process B11.) Time will vary up to 30 minutes or more for each person. Time taken with this process will free up the group to work synergistically, quickly and creatively in approaching and completing the task.

Process: As an uninterrupted round, invite participants to share any thoughts, feelings, body sensations and events which are present and, if expressed, may add to the group or, if unexpressed, may detract from participation in the group. For example:

My daughter had a baby last night. It is our first grandchild.
I saw an accident on the way here, and I'm still shaken up.
I broke an expensive piece of equipment yesterday and haven't reported it yet. I'm worried about it.

I'm giving a presentation to a client today and I'm feeling nervous.

*I was acknowledged this morning by the CEO for my part in the
    policy review process. It was neat.*

*I had an argument with Bill (also in group) and am feeling uncom-
    fortable around him. I request a clearing session (in the group
    now or at an arranged time outside the group).*

All members give full attention to the speaker. The facilitator
may coach people if they appear stuck or incomplete.
Interventions could include:

Is there anything else you'd like to share about that?

Can you say some more about that?

How is that for you?

Is there any support you would like to request?

Are you now fully present?

*Is there something you need to do (right now or after the meeting)
    about that?*

Continue with the round until all members have had the
opportunity to share.

At the completion of the round declare the round complete
and move on to the next process or task.

Variation:

☐ In larger groups it is often more practical to do this exercise
   in pairs, threes or subgroups, with an opportunity for a few
   people to share in the whole group afterwards.

B13 Getting Complete

This exercise is powerful as an ongoing process as well as essential when ending a group.

Purpose: To provide an occasion for group members to complete their involvement with a group, a group project or a particular issue, and to ensure that no extra baggage is taken away from the group.

Time: Up to 5 minutes per person.

Process: Ask each person in turn:

What do you need to say to complete your involvement with this group? or
What do you need to say to be complete?

Then:

Is there anything else? Any thoughts, feelings, unmet expectations, requests, promises, acknowledgments? (Suggest as appropriate.)
If there is anything that you might say to someone after the group is over, I request you say it now.

The person looks to see if he or she has any baggage to leave behind; anything he or she would say to someone else after the group.

Are there any acknowledgments that anyone would like to make of themselves or others?
The only response from those acknowledged is a simple *Thank you.*

B14 Speaking the Higher Purpose

This process uses the *holonomic principle* explained by John Heron on pages 222 to 224..

Purpose: To find out the higher purpose of the group.

Time: 30 minutes, but depends on size of group.

Process: Explain the holonomic principle, which asserts that the whole is represented in the part. Just as one small part of a holographic picture contains the entire hologram so one person in a group will often identify an issue for the whole group. Allow the group to explore the possibility of using non-rational processes as a valid alternative to more traditional methods. If people are skeptical, encourage them to suspend belief and act as if it will really work. The method for this ritual process is to discover one person who will speak the higher purpose of the group.

Have participants relax and center themselves. Suggest they close their eyes and concentrate on their breathing. Instruct them to breathe into their bellies and relax a little each time they exhale.

When the group is relaxed, have each member place a small identifiable object, such as a watch, ring or earring, into a hat. Without looking inside the hat the facilitator takes out one object, then gives it and the hat to the owner of the object. That member takes out another object and gives it and the hat to its owner, and so on.

The last person to receive his or her object is the *holonomic focus,* the group spokesperson, and is asked to put the ritual hat on. The spokesperson centers himself or herself, taking as much time as necessary and using whatever method he or she chooses.

The facilitator then asks: "What is the higher purpose of this group?"

After the spokesperson has responded, complete the ritual with something like a group circle in which the hat is passed and put on by each member. During this circle, ensure that the spokesperson deroles.

Variation: There are many possible variations on this exercise—such as having the spokesperson answer questions. See the John Heron interview, pages 217 to 230.

Facilitators' Training Program

Introduction

Here is a program outline which you can use as a peer-training program for facilitators. The purpose of this program is to develop facilitation skills through experiential learning. Each of the first nine sessions is based on one or two chapters of this book. Sessions 10 and 11 are to be designed by the participants. Session 12 is for self- and peer assessment, and planning for further training.

This is an advanced training program suitable for people who already have experience in group work as participants and preferably some experience as facilitators.

The program will work well with a group of 6 to 12. If there are 6 people, there will be time for plenty of discussion. If more than 12 people take part, the program will need to be modified and/or the time for each exercise extended.

Resources

- ☐ *The Zen of Groups*
- ☐ Whiteboard
- ☐ Large newsprint sheets.
- ☐ Whiteboard pens and felt-tipped pens.
- ☐ Notebook for each person.
- ☐ A large room in which you can move around easily.

Sessions

Total time: 36 hours plus 2-hour preparatory meeting plus arranged outing.

12 three-hour sessions, or

8 three-hour sessions plus 2 full-day sessions (6 hours + lunch break).

Preparatory session

It is essential to have a 2-hour preparatory session so that proposed participants can:

Meet one another.

Share their specific purpose for taking part in the program.

Arrange where and when the training sessions will be held.

Commit themselves to full participation and attendance at every session.

Set ground rules—such as, confidentiality, punctuality, being coachable.

Address any housekeeping issues which need to be organized in advance.

Clarify and confirm who will be in the program.

Decide who will facilitate the first session.

> *It is suggested that one person be the primary facilitator for each session. Individual sections in each session can also be subcontracted to other participants to facilitate.*

Getting the learning and facilitator feedback

An opportunity for getting the learning and giving feedback to each facilitator can be built into each session by taking five minutes at the end of each exercise for reflection and self- and peer assessment.

The process gives two minutes for the trainee facilitator, who completes the sentences:

What I noticed was . . .
What I learned was . . .

This is followed by three minutes for the participants who each complete the sentences:

What I learned was . . .
My constructive criticism/acknowledgment to you (the trainee facilitator) is . . .

Encourage short, pithy comments. Discourage stories, discussion or justification. Encourage participants to receive feedback as a gift, whether they agree with it or not.

Criteria for effective facilitation

Criteria for effective facilitation are developed as part of Session 4 of this training program. These criteria can take the form of characteristics/qualities or competencies (what a facilitator can do). They then become a checklist for facilitator feedback for the following sessions and the basis of a self- and peer assessment process in Session 12.

Session 1: Preparing the Ground

Preparation: Read through all of the Facilitators' Training Program and Chapter 1, Preparing the Ground.

Session outline
A (30 minutes):

Welcome everyone to the first session and introduce yourself. (Give a short background of your experience and share something personal.)

Introductory exercise—choose from *The Zen of Groups* Toolkit: Tools for the First Session of a New Group.

Outline the session program to the group.

Choose a timekeeper for the rest of the session.

B (30 minutes):
Clarify the purpose of training program.

Use a round in which each person speaks the purpose in his or her own words.

Write down key words from each person on large sheets of paper.

At the end of the round, identify any agreement and disagreement, and align the group on a common purpose.

Write this out and have everyone write it down.

C (30 minutes):

Choose a trust-building exercise from *The Zen of Groups* Toolkit: Tools for Developing Trust and Group Identity.

D (50 minutes):
Sharing on Chapter 1, Preparing the Ground

Have someone introduce the chapter and give a summary (10 minutes).

Use a round, structured or unstructured—each person speaking with a time limit, say 3 minutes, on what he or she got out of the chapter. Then have a general discussion on the chapter.

E (10 minutes):

Prepare a schedule for each person to facilitate one or more of the sessions of the program.

F (30 minutes):

Give homework for the next session—read Chapter 2, Facilitating Yourself.

Confirm the next facilitator.

Ask for feedback on the session in two rounds—the first of constructive criticism, and the second on affirmation and acknowledgment. Ask the participants to be specific.

Aspects to consider in the feedback:

- ☐ Is everyone present?
- ☐ Were time limits, including starting and finishing on time, kept?
- ☐ Did everyone participate fully?
- ☐ Was the group purpose clarified?
- ☐ What level of trust has been generated?
- ☐ What was the key learning for each person?
- ☐ What were the strengths and areas for improvement of the facilitation?
- ☐ Acknowledgments of everyone's participation.
- ☐ Any withholds (things you might say to someone else about the group afterwards) need to be said now.

End the session.

Session 2: Facilitating Ourselves

Preparation: Read Chapter 2, Facilitating Yourself

Session outline
A (15 minutes):

Welcome the group and introduce yourself.
Outline the session program.
Choose a timekeeper.
Getting fully present:

*Is there anything you need to say to be fully present in the group
now?* (2 minutes each.) (See Getting Fully Present, Process
B12, page 164.)

B (45 minutes):

Exercise from *The Zen of Groups,* Tool 38, My Most
Precious Possession.

C (1 hour):
Sharing on Chapter 2, Facilitating Yourself

Have someone introduce the chapter and give a summary
(10 minutes).
Then have a round, each person speaking (3 minutes) on his or
her response to the chapter.
Follow with a general discussion.

D (30 minutes):

Have the group divide into pairs. One person of each pair
explores the questions below. The other person listens
without comment, taking notes if requested.
Questions:

In what areas of my life am I the most self-facilitative?
(3 minutes each)
In what areas of my life am I the least self-facilitative?
(2 minutes each)
*What is one area in which I would like to become more self-facilita-
tive? What will this look like? What's one step I can take within
the next 24 hours towards this?* (5 minutes each)

Swap roles and repeat.

Bring the whole group together and ask participants to share
their discoveries (10 minutes).

E (10 minutes):

Set up a buddy system.

Participants contract in pairs to coach one another, by tele-
phone or in person, at least twice before the next session.
Have them arrange times and write them in their diaries.

F (20 minutes):

Homework reminder—read Chapter 3, Facilitating Others.
Confirm the next facilitator.
Ask for feedback on the session—see Session 1.

End the session.

Session 3: Facilitating Others

Preparation: Read Chapter 3, Facilitating Others.

Session outline
A (20 minutes):

Welcome the group and introduce yourself.
Outline the session program.
Choose a timekeeper.
Process B12, Getting Fully Present, page 164 (2 minutes each).
Review the buddy system:
How is it working?
What's missing?
Any requests and promises?

B (20 minutes):

Process B1, Being with Another, page 141 (5 minutes each way).
Sharing in large group, have a round on:
What I saw from this process was . . .

C (25 minutes):
Sharing on Chapter 3 in the whole group.

D (25 minutes):
Process B7, Identity Check, page 151.

Participants choose a partner to whom they have a strong response, positive or negative.
Allow 5 minutes each way.
Repeat the process with a new partner, then ask participants to share in the whole group.

E (1 hour):

Process B3, My World, Your World, page 144.

F (30 minutes):

Homework reminder—read Chapter 4, Facilitating a Group
Also remind participants about contacting their buddies.
Confirm the next facilitator.
Feedback on the session—see Session 1.
Process B13, Getting Complete, page 166 (2 minutes each).

End the session.

Session 4: Facilitating a Group

Preparation: Read Chapter 4, Facilitating a Group

Session outline
A (1 hour):

Welcome the group and introduce yourself.
Outline the session program.
Choose a timekeeper.
Sharing Withholds, Tool 30, from *The Zen of Groups*, or Group
Clearing, Process 11b, page 161.
Note: By this session there will be plenty of "baggage"
emerging in the group. Revise session program if more
time is needed.

B (1 hour):
Sharing on Chapter 4, Facilitating a Group.

Brainstorm in the whole group (see *The Zen of Groups*, Tool 3)
What are the characteristics of an effective facilitator?

Prioritize the resulting list (see *The Zen of Groups*, Tool 10,
Priority-setting).

Note: Keep this list and use as criteria in Session 12.

Working in pairs or threes and using the prioritized list, have
participants address the following questions:
What are my strengths as a facilitator?
What are my weaknesses?
What are my areas of training and development?

Ask participants to design some specific actions to forward
their training and development for this week.

C (30 minutes):

Share in the whole group, as an unstructured round (see *The Zen of Groups*, Tool 1), answers to this question:

What synergistic experiences have I had?

Ask participants to consider all the group experiences they have had: family, school, work, recreation, community and spiritual.

D (30 minutes):

Review the buddy system.
Homework reminder—read Chapter 5, On the Edge of the Sword.
Confirm the next facilitator.
Feedback on the session—see Session 1.
Process B13, Getting complete, page 166.

End the session.

Session 5: On the Edge of the Sword
(using interventions)

Preparation: Read Chapter 5, On the Edge of the Sword

Session outline
A (30 minutes):

Welcome the group and introduce yourself.
Outline the session program.
Choose a timekeeper.
Process B12, Getting Fully Present, page 164.
Process B2, Being with a Group, page 142.

B (30 minutes):

Sharing on Chapter 5, On the Edge of the Sword.

Ask participants to share with the whole group their answers to this question:

What is the attitude of the facilitator when using interventions?

In other words, where is he or she coming from? Who is he or she being?

C (1 hour):

Working as a whole group, ask participants to choose three sections in the chapter and develop role plays based on them.

Allow 20 minutes for each role play, including setting up, presenting, deroling and sharing in the whole group.

See Process B9, Role Plays, page 153.

D (30 minutes):

Acknowledgment.

> Choose a tool from *The Zen of Groups*, Tools for Affirmation and Acknowledgment.

E (30 minutes):

> Homework reminder—read Chapter 6, Working on the Different Levels.
>
> Confirm the next facilitator.
>
> Feedback on the session—see Session 1.
>
> Process B13, Getting Complete, page 166.

End the session.

Session 6: Working on the Different Levels

Preparation: Read Chapter 6, Working on the Different Levels.

Session outline
A (30 minutes):

Bring a welcoming ritual to start the session. Allow 10 minutes.
Welcome the group and introduce yourself.
Outline the session program.
Choose a timekeeper.
Choose an exercise from *The Zen of Groups*, Tools for
Energizing the Group (5 minutes).
Process B12, Getting Fully Present, page 164.

B (30 minutes):

Have participants share their thoughts on Chapter 6, Working
on the Different Levels (see Session 1D).
Then ask participants to address these questions in pairs:

Which levels do I feel most comfortable with?

Which levels do I feel the least at home with?

Are there any levels which I would remove or add?

Finish with a round of sharing in the whole group.

C (30 minutes):

Tool 48, Feelings Continuum, from *The Zen of Groups*.

D (20 minutes):

Tool 58, Mind Expander, from *The Zen of Groups*.

E (10 minutes):

Ask participants to share in a round what they have noticed about changing energy levels during parts C and D above.

F (30 minutes):

Review the training program so far.

This is the halfway point.
Use Soft evaluation model No. 2, page 139.
Have participants work in pairs or threes, writing down their responses. Finish with a group sharing.

G (30 minutes):

Homework reminder—read Chapter 7, Getting to Agreement, and Chapter 8, Cutting Through, to the middle of page 83.
Feedback—see Session 1.
As a group, design and carry out an ending ritual. Have one that reflects the uniqueness of your group.

End the session.

Session 7: Getting to Agreement and Cutting Through

Preparation: Read Chapter 7, Getting to Agreement, and Chapter 8, Cutting Through, to middle of page 83.

Session outline
A (10 minutes):

Welcome the group and introduce yourself.
Outline the session program.
Choose a timekeeper.
Process B12, Getting Fully Present, page 164 (in pairs, 2 minutes each way).
Have participants complete with existing buddy, then choose a new buddy who will be rigorous in interrupting their patterns.

B (30 minutes):
Sharing on Chapter 7 and 8 up to the middle of page of 83.

Have someone introduce the chapters and give a summary (10 minutes).
Follow with a general plan.

C (40 minutes):
Getting to agreement and barriers to agreement.

Ask participants to plan a group event or outing to be held this week. Remind them that they will need to agree on what is done, the date and time, cost, and where they will meet.
Also stress that everyone must attend as part of the training.
Refer to Meeting Design, page 120.

Have two people monitor the barriers to agreement which arise (see pages 72 to 75). Wrtie the barriers on the whiteboard as they occur. For the last 10 minutes of this section, debrief the process and how any barriers were dismantled.

D (40 minutes):
Sabotage

Have participants work in pairs, taking 5 minutes each way to coach one another on how they sabotage themselves everyday. Stress to participants that they should be direct. Do not allow any time extension. Do not share in the whole group.

Go straight on to a round in the whole group addressing the question:

How do I sabotage this and other groups?
(We all have our ways and means?

If a person has trouble identifying sabotage patterns, coach them. This will be a breakthrough for you. Be rigorous and yet light. Look back to their patterns you have noticed in earlier sessions. (Divide 30 minutes by the number of people in the group and set individual time limits.)

E (30 minutes):
Blaming and scapegoating

Note: This is a powerful exercise and can bring up strong feelings and catharsis (crying, anger and fear) for some participants as they flip into other situations which they find triggering.

Do some physical energizers from Tool 64 of *The Zen of Groups* (5 minutes).

Find a large cushion and put it in the middle of the group circle. Ask the group to choose a name (not the same as anyone in the group) for the cushion. Have participants stand up in a circle about 3 feet away from the cushion (for our purposes, called Bruce). Encourage them to give themselves full permission to blame Bruce for everything that hasn't worked in the training group since it began.

It's all Bruce's fault. He caused everything to go wrong, and what's more he did it on purpose. He is not aligned with the group and is unrepentant. Encourage participants to shout and yell at Bruce, laugh at him behind his back, make snide comments to him or about him and be mean to him. He is their scapegoat and they can project all their dissatisfactions onto him, really exaggerating their anger and upset. Keep this going for 5 to 10 minutes.

Ask participants to stop, sit down in the circle and share. Allow 15 minutes to explore this important issue. Suggest participants focus on:

☐ The things I like about blaming and scapegoating.
☐ The things I dislike about blaming and scapegoating.
☐ What is really going on? (Not being responsible and accountable ourselves.)

If people have become activated, allow them to continue to vent while the discussion takes place or give them some group time. Encourage the group to attend to them through the gift of free attention rather than intervention. Just ask the person if there is anything he or she wants to say or do. Give him or her physical support only if they ask for it. When ready, get the activated person to derole the cushion (how is it not like Bruce?) and give it a hug (see Process B9).

F (30 minutes):

Exercise: Have a group scream (1 minute).

Homework reminder—pages 83 to 90 of Chapter 8, Cutting Through.

Review the buddy system.

Feedback—see Session 1.

Confirm the next facilitator.

You may want to incorporate your ending ritual from Session 6 for this and following sessions.

End the session.

Session 8: Cutting Through

Preparation: Read pages 83 to 90 of Chapter 8, Cutting Through.

Session outline
A (25 minutes):

Welcome the group and introduce yourself.
Outline the session program.
Choose a timekeeper.
Process B12, Getting Fully Present, page 164 (in pairs, 2 minutes each way).
Conduct a debriefing on the outing (15 minutes).
Address the following questions:

What behaviors did I notice?
☐ Facilitating myself.
☐ Facilitating one another.
☐ Facilitating the group.
☐ Disempowering myself, others and the group.
☐ Giving advice, blaming, coaching without agreement.

How does my behavior within the group differ from my behavior outside the group?

B (30 minutes):
Sharing on Chapter 8, pages 83 to 90, Groupthink and Challenging.

Have someone introduce the material and give a summary (10 minutes).
Then have a round, each person speaking for 3 minutes on his or her response to the chapter.
Follow with a general discussion if there is time.

Keep to this process.

Have a timekeeper monitor the times. Manage the time rigorously.

C (15 minutes):

Groupthink

Brainstorm

What is special about this group? (3 minutes)

Then ask participants to choose another group to compare themselves with and brainstorm:

We are better than (the other) group because . . . (3 minutes).

Finish with a round on what the group noticed. For example, had they already decided they were better during the first brainstorm? Where is the line between being special and being better?

Discuss the issues raised in Groupthink, pages 83 to 85.

D (20 minutes):

Have participants move into three subgroups, with each group taking one of these topics.

1. Challenges within the group.
2. The facilitator challenging the group.
3. Challenges to the facilitator.

Ask each group to design processes or role plays for the whole group to practice these scenarios. Encourage rotation of roles so that several people get the opportunity to be in the key roles.

E (75 minutes):

Give each subgroup 25 minutes to work with the whole group. Include a 5-minute debriefing to draw out the learning.

F (15 minutes):

Homework reminder—read Chapters 9, Facilitation and the Client, and 10, Facilitation and Change, and Tool A1, Workshop Design.

Remind participants to contact their buddies.

Feedback—see Session 1.

Confirm the next facilitator.

Process B13, Getting Complete, page 166.

The closing ritual.

End the session.

Session 9: Facilitation and the Client, Facilitation and Change, and Workshop Design

Preparation: Read Chapter 9, Facilitation and the Client, Chapter 10, Facilitation and Change, and Tool A1, Workshop Design.

Session outline
A (30 minutes):

Welcome the group and introduce yourself.

Outline the session program.

Choose a timekeeper.

Have a clearing round, perhaps Tool 30 Sharing Withholds, from *The Zen of Groups*.

B (40 minutes):

Sharing on Chapters 9 and 10.

Have someone introduce the material and give a summary (10 minutes).

Then have a round, each person speaking for 3 minutes on his or her response to the chapters.

Follow with a general discussion if there is time. Keep to this process and have a timekeeper monitor the times. Manage the round rigorously.

C (30 minutes):

Tool 54, Building the Group Vision, from *The Zen of Groups* as guide to discovering the *higher purpose* of the group.

D (1 hour):

Form the whole group into two subgroups. Subgroup A will
design Session 10 of this training program, and subgroup B
will design Session 11.

Use Tool A1, Workshop Design, and any facilitative processes
necessary (from this book as well as from *The Zen Of
Groups*). Each subgroup is to develop a written design of the
training program on a large sheet of paper. Their design
should clearly outline the sections and give processes and
times.

The focus for session 10 is *Synergy*.
The focus for session 11 is *Empowerment*.

E (20 minutes):

Feedback—see Session 1.

There may need to be a homework reminder, depending on the
content of the next session.

Confirm the next facilitator.

Process B13, Getting Complete, page 166.

The closing ritual.

End of session.

Session 10: Synergy

As designed by a subgroup during Session 9. There may need to be a homework reminder, depending on the content of the next session.

Session 11: Empowerment

As designed by a subgroup during Session 9.
Homework reminder—read Tool 92, Self- and Peer Assessment from *The Zen Of Groups*.

Session 12: Self- and Peer Assessment and Further Training.

Preparation: Read Self- and Peer Assessment, Tool 92 in *The Zen of Groups*.

Session outline
A (15 minutes):

Welcome the group and introduce yourself.
Outline the session program.
Choose a timekeeper.
Process B12, Getting Fully Present, page 164 (in pairs, 2 minutes each way).

B (2 hours):

Tool 92 Self- and Peer Assessment, from *The Zen of Groups*.

There will need to be some time limits set for each person unless everyone agrees to extend the time of this session. Use the criteria developed in Session 4.

C (30 minutes):

Follow-up and action-planning session.

The two questions below can be addressed in several ways—in pairs, in threes and in a whole-group discussion.

Where do we go from here?
What do we want to invent that will further our own training in line with our vision?

D (15 minutes):

Process B13, Getting Complete, page 166. Celebrate yourselves together. The training program has ended.

Part 3

Interviews

Dale Hunter

I'm a facilitator and mediator, specializing in organizational development and community development. I work within organizations and I also facilitate public meetings and workshops which involve the public. I particularly enjoy conflict resolution, as well as strategic planning and team building.

How did you begin doing these jobs?
There were probably two main strands which came together. One was my work in community development and organizational development with the city council. I became involved in facilitating workshops and meetings in the community and among the staff within the council.

The other main strand was the personal-development work I undertook for myself, which involved a lot of different training programs. I also became a trainer in a personal-development method called *co-counseling*. I became more and more interested in what people could achieve in a cooperative group, and the possibilities of facilitation and group synergy.

Tell me about synergy.
I noticed that there were times when a group would be particularly effective—effective beyond what seemed to be reasonably possible. There seems to be an energy available that a group can tap into at times that has it be supereffective. I became very, very interested in what it takes to tap into this supereffective energy—or what we call *synergy*—and the possibility of synergy for all groups.

*When you say **synergy** you don't just mean the group getting something done, you mean something a bit more?*
Yes. It's both getting something done, and the way it achieves that; and it's also how it has people be with one another and with other people outside the group. It has to do with the *domain of being* and being with people in such a way that more becomes available.

Is it something like a win-win solution, but for a whole group?
Yes. It seems that we can be much more in groups than you or I can be individually. Together we can tap into an energy which encourages us to be much more than individuals.

As I understand it, a key concept of facilitation is helping a group reach consensus or a decision that everyone is happy with.
Yes, facilitation is about guiding the process of a cooperative group. Facilitation was developed to help cooperative groups or peer groups reach decisions and take action on them. So consensus or collective decision-making is an integral part of cooperacy. The committee structure is designed for majority decision-making and is an integral part of democracy.

Could we use collective decision-making in a much wider context than we do now?
Yes, I believe we can use it a lot more. What keeps us from doing this is that not enough of us have the skills to bring a group to consensus. If the skills were widely known and widely practiced, groups would feel much more comfortable with working cooperatively.

Presumably a lot of the skills you need in a cooperative group would be very helpful in a democratic group?
Yes. If you look closely at how a democratic group works, particularly a committee, an effective chairperson will spend quite a lot of time endeavoring to reach a consensus before a motion is put and a vote taken. The skills aren't totally separate.

There is quite a strong element of confrontation in the committee structure—it thrives on the cut and thrust of confrontation and factionalism. In a cooperative group, different views are also important, but the way they are worked through is somewhat different.

One of the criticisms you hear is that collective decision-making takes too much time.
Without skills it does take time. With skills it can be very quick. Collective decision-making sometimes does take longer than majority decision-making, but often the decisions stick better.

So what you're saying is that decisions reached by democratic decision-making can be very quick, but there is often an aftermath with people muttering and not carrying the decision out. And this can mean the consensus method may have been quicker in the long run?
Yes.

How do you work as a facilitator in organizational development? Can you give me some examples of facilitation affecting the culture of an organization?
A couple of examples spring to mind. One of them is the city council where I worked for 13 years. I was involved in a wide-scale internal-participation process looking at what the organization needed to be in the future after the reform of local government. It was a facilitated process, facilitated on various levels with staff meetings, working parties and workshops which touched everyone in the organization—1100 people.

The process was guided by a consultative team drawn from all levels of the organization and working closely with the city manager. This led to a very big alteration in the make-up of the organization and included the development of a charter, change-management and performance-management programs, and the setting up of different networks. It had a marked effect on the culture of the organization. People became much more empowered—able to speak up, to say what they thought needed to be changed and to have some faith that action would be taken on their suggestions. There was better communication throughout the organization—a change in the whole atmosphere.

It began with an initial management working party. I was chairperson and we actually restructured ourselves as a cooperative working party with management, staff and union representatives, and brought in an outside facilitator to keep it more as a cooperative group. Then we developed staff participation processes and training workshops, and I facilitated many of these. It was a large-scale program where there were a number of facilitators.

But the basic driving force was this cooperative group?
Yes. The cooperative working party represented the main strands of the organization. It was a large group, varying from 18 to 20 people at its biggest.

And this went on for how long?
The initial term was for three years but the big change I saw happening was in the first two years.

And did this result in efficiencies for the council?
Yes, dramatic efficiencies. All sorts of things came out of the process—procedures that didn't work which had been known about by staff for a long time but which nothing had been done about. A classic example was the storeroom, from which all the laborers collected their equipment. This opened at 7:30 AM but the workers all started at 7:00, so they'd have to get all their tools out the night before. If they couldn't do what they planned to do, they'd have to wait around for half an hour to get other tools.

This had been going on for something like 20 years and involved about 500 laborers. It was changed in one day when the working party went directly to the city manager. This was a big alteration in efficiency for those 500 people.

Another place where I've recently seen a shift within the culture of an organization is at another city council, where we've been training people in how to be effective in meetings. We've now held workshops which have been attended by about 100 staff. In the last one or two I've noticed quite a marked shift in the general understanding of how groups work in meetings. It seems clear there have been enough people trained to have altered the way meetings work in the organization and that skills have been picked up by others before they attended our workshops. There does seem to be a cumulative effect in working with an organization—if you reach enough people, some things will start to shift.

Facilitative processes are very much a part of the total quality management movement affecting most organizations. It is recognized that people need to be involved in constant quality improvement, with improvements being driven upwards as much as downwards. The whole facilitative style empowers people to say what needs to happen and to make suggestions, and it's proven again and again that it encourages people to be proactive.

What is the difference between a facilitator and a trainer?
A facilitator doesn't need to know anything about the content of a meeting. A facilitator is a process guide and is there to make it easy for the group to achieve what it sets out to do. His or her role is to empower the group, and one of the basic ideas is that the wisdom is contained within the group. It's a matter of the group tapping into its own wisdom and potential, and the role of the facilitator is to aid that process.

A trainer is more interested in transferring skills and passing on knowledge and understanding or straight information to people. There's a different emphasis. It's based more on: "I know, and my job at the end of this process is to ensure that you know too." So it's coming from a different place.

In your job don't you fulfill both roles? When you teach facilitation you would be the trainer, teaching people how to facilitate?
Yes, that's true. Training people in facilitation skills needs to be largely experiential. A good way for people to train as facilitators is for them to take on an apprentice role to an experienced facilitator. They learn by watching another facilitator work and asking questions, and getting more understanding that way.

Who does a facilitator need to be?
This is probably the secret to being an effective facilitator. It's not so much what you do or what you say, because words can be said in so many different ways. It's more to do with who you are and who you are being for the group you're working with. There are different ways of saying that: where you are coming from or what your attitude is. The relationship you develop with the group is the key to effective facilitation. There is a body of skills, but the bottom line is: "Who are you for the group?"

Would this tie in with what you said before about the wisdom being contained in the group—a facilitator is the person in the group who knows that the group knows the answer?
Definitely. That's a key one and new facilitators often fall into the trap that they need to know the answer when a difficult issue is being worked through within the group. A facilitator doesn't need to know anything in terms of the content to facilitate the group. It's not that the facilitator doesn't know anything, but he or she doesn't need to know anything about the content of the discussion to facilitate the group.

The facilitator's role has a lot to do with honoring and respecting people as individuals, encouraging them to be their most powerful, contributive and effective selves, and also making allowances for each one's baggage. When any baggage is seen to be disempowering for the group, the facilitator cuts through it so it doesn't get in the way of the group as a whole.

There's also a spiritual dimension. We're all spiritual beings operating in this world and we have certain ways of behaving, some of which are productive and some counterproductive. The facilitator works with these behaviors, but is always honoring the whole person or the spiritual beings in the group. That might sound a bit esoteric but that's really what it's all about.

The facilitator looks only at what's happening and not at the decisions being reached?
That's up to each facilitator and his or her values. For example, I wouldn't facilitate a group that's involved in violent action. That would be against my values. So it's important for a facilitator to be aware of his or her own values. If you honor and respect people, it's unlikely you would want to take violent action.

I've never been called on to facilitate a group involved in violent action. But I've certainly facilitated groups which have come up with decisions that I don't agree with or wouldn't want to be part of. That doesn't matter because, as the facilitator, I was not involved in the content or the subsequent action.

I've often been involved in clarifying the wording of decisions if they're not totally clear. That is part of the facilitator's role. And there are different styles of facilitation. It is useful for a facilitator to challenge a decision if he or she feels it is against the group's own values.

Have you facilitated groups where you have been a member of the group being facilitated?

Yes. Lots of facilitation happens this way and it's fine as long as you put aside your desire to be involved in the content while you are facilitating. One way you can minimize this conflict is to rotate the role of facilitator among group members. As more people learn facilitation skills, this will become more common and practical.

I see it as very useful in society for more and more people to have these skills. We are part of groups all our lives—extended family groups, work groups, sports groups—and the effectiveness of these can be greatly enhanced by all the members knowing facilitation skills.

> **The facilitator's role has a lot to do with honoring and respecting people as individuals.**

Anne Bailey

Tell me about your background in groups and in facilitating groups.

I am, and have always been, delighted by the energy generated when people come together for a creative purpose. Currently, I facilitate individuals, organizations, project and special interest groups.

The first groups I remember go back to the playground at school when I was about five. One of the things I loved to do at playtime was to link arms with one or two other girls and go off around the playground saying: "Who wants to play cowboys and Indians" or whatever it was, and we would do this for most of the playtime, gathering up increasing numbers of children. This seemed to be the game itself—just going around inviting people to play, and the group kept getting bigger and bigger.

And then in small groups we made up plays and we'd act out stories. Usually we'd find a story we liked and we'd keep doing that same one. I remember one of the teachers getting us to go through the school performing this play, and it was like having our playtime over and over again in front of all the big kids. In various forms, that kept happening through my whole primary schooling—a small group of people working together and producing something.

My next group experience that stands out would be when I led a Sunday School class. We decided we were going to raise money for something that had appealed to us and we were very successful. It was no trouble to do it—it was something we all wanted to do and it just happened—it wasn't hard work at all.

Can you remember anything about facilitating in those particular groups?
Well, I guess I did facilitate it because the other children were quite a lot younger than myself. I encouraged people to say what they thought about different ideas and what tasks they would take on. It was a lot to do with not imposing things on people—allowing things to rise from within the group.

So from early on, you've worked in what we might call the facilitative way?
Yes. As a facilitator, what I'm looking at, or inviting out, is the essence of individuals. When I'm facilitating a group, like a personal-development group, that's what I'm speaking to. I'm speaking to the part of a person that responds to life—the life-enhancing part of a person. There was something about my early training within a church context that really encouraged and developed that.

Later I went to a teachers' college and took quite a strong role in social activities. I started a group at college within the Student Christian Movement. We investigated semi-political issues around college life and around the implications of education. A group of us worked together and became a strong force at the college. And we had an itinerant leader who went around to all the colleges and universities, supporting people who were leading groups. She would meet with us every two months and we'd plan what we were going to do together.

I went to one of their conferences and had the experience of being in a large group where the leader stretched our ideas in a challenging way but in a way they wanted to go. It was like having a catalyst. In my work as a facilitator, I am looking to be a catalyst for something that wants to happen. That's a theme for me as a facilitator: What *wants* to happen here?

*What groups are you working with now, and how are you
working with facilitation?*

One of the groups I've been working with is a group of older
women, 55 plus. They came together because they were
depressed, or a partner or close relative had died, or they were
just looking for contact with others. Working with them has been
an amazing exploration—it's been a fabulous group to work with.

And once again it's very much been about allowing people the
space to listen to each other, and highlighting and drawing out
the enlivening responses. The group has moved from being quite
reserved and not very aware of itself as a group into one where
people do things together outside group time. They formed a
separate social group called the Gloom Busters. They go out to
lunch and to the movies, they go dancing and they play cards.

Was there a particular focus for the group?

It's basically a support group. It has to do with looking at the
strong issues for women of that age—relationships with family,
dealing with attitudes towards death, people's life stories and
forgiveness.

*You were involved in assertiveness training in the early '70s,
weren't you?*

When my children were very young there were hardly any activities for young children. There was only one kindergarten with a
long waiting list, and there were virtually no facilities for women.
I was encouraged by a community worker to start a play group.
So women with children of preschool age came together and we
found there were things that we, as adults, wanted to do too. It
evolved into several of us training as assertiveness leaders.

It was really good learning for me although at first I didn't
think I was doing a good job. I'd come away from the sessions
thinking: "I'm no good at this. I don't even know that I want to

do it"—and giving myself a hard time about it. It was partly because I was dealing with a frontier—at that stage assertiveness courses weren't common. We were asking people to look for uncomfortable situations and find alternative behaviors. But I just kept on doing it and gradually leading the sessions became easier and easier. I find being assertive is an important aspect of being both a member and a facilitator of a group.

My focus has become more career-oriented in terms of actually facilitating in a broader way—supporting people individually and collectively to discover what it is they really would like to see happen for themselves, particularly professionally, and then supporting them to set up a structure for that to occur.

So you have done that for groups and individuals?
Yes—I really love working that way.

Another theme for me is that anything is possible. If someone is really passionate about something, then that is the thing to do. And there are always ways of having things work.

In what other ways have you used facilitation recently?
There's a neighborhood women's drop-in group that wanted to meet for a variety of reasons: wanting company, wanting stimulation, wanting to explore issues, just wanting to have time out—all kinds of reasons. I facilitated this group informally—we found the main thing was to have time to talk about what was going on for them, and to be able to relax and laugh and enjoy each other. That was the purpose of the group.

I've also been working on some specific training programs with local groups. We were working with having people explore what it takes to have their work meetings be effective—looking at what stops them from having the meetings be totally successful.

That's more like training?
Yes, it's more like training, but it's done in a facilitative style. It's done by participants looking at their own experience and drawing out the learnings from that. There is some content but it's more to do with people actually stretching their own boundaries beyond what they've done previously.

You mentioned facilitative style. What to you is a facilitative style? What would you contrast it with?
Well, it's obviously contrasted with chalk and talk. My theory is that a facilitator is not there to provide input or content but as the guardian of the group getting what it wants. It's like a watchdog, a resource to help the group achieve its purpose—keeping the group on track, providing stimulation or suggestions when that's necessary—being like a warrior for the group.

So facilitation is about drawing out of the group rather than telling the group?
Yes. It's also encouraging or supporting the group to identify certain aspects about itself or certain qualities that individuals have or certain qualities that a group has. Sometimes it's making the slightly invisible visible. I really like the hologram concept. A new group doesn't have a particular individual identity, but as the group meets and develops, its identity becomes clearer and clearer. That doesn't mean to say it's going to stay the same; it's probably going to change. But its identity does become increasingly clear.

What happens in a group is connected to how willing and able its members are to make themselves available for what can happen when they start working together. It has to do with being willing to participate in a process and trusting the people you're working with or trusting a process and knowing that something unexpected will occur—something that none of the individuals could have come up with alone.

Something unique is created when people cooperate whole-heartedly. For me, it has to do with people allowing what I'd call love. I don't know whether that's the right term for it—there are lots of ways you could identify it—but I identify it as love.

In writing The Zen of Groups, one of your purposes was to help groups achieve synergy. Could you talk a bit about synergy?
I often experience synergy when we three authors work together. I experience it in other groups, too, in flashes, moments, periods of time or events when everything just clicks. What to me is really exciting and challenging and quite scary is to work with people where that's what's expected.

When I meet with Bill and Dale, I expect that what comes out will be like a new creation. My experience is that there's something to attend to between us if that's not occurring—something's getting in the way. Often it's something one of us hasn't said to another—thoughts or ideas that we're withholding.

And is that your experience of other groups, too; that the with-holds are what stifles the group?
Yes, this is often true. It is vital for a facilitator to be aware when someone is withholding.

Tell us about your training and your feeling about training.
A strong training influence on me has been my mother. She was an incredibly permission-giving person. She never said anything derogatory about anybody and always saw people very compassionately. So that has always been part of my life, in ways I don't even recognize, and that's been the backbone of how I function as a facilitator.

One of the most important aspects of working as a facilitator is to put myself into training and development on a regular basis. It gives me fresh experience in giving up what I already know for what I don't know—keeping my own sword sharp.

Bill Taylor

Tell me about your background in groups and facilitating groups.
One of the first was an extremely non-facilitative role in military training. I was a warrant officer in the school cadet corps and was in charge of the NCOs' training unit. I had to take boys—just a little younger than me—and train them to be lance-corporals, corporals and sergeants. This consisted of drilling them—yelling at them mostly. I learned the way to get ahead in the military world was to yell very loudly and authoritatively. So one of my first experience of groups was, if you shouted loudly, people did what you told them.

Did you have any other early experiences which were not quite so autocratic—maybe some older men who impressed you?
Two men come to mind. One was my Bible-class teacher. Although he was in charge it never felt as though he was. Anybody could say anything—it felt very open. Anybody could talk, yet he moved it along. I learned a lot from him.

The other man was a boss I had when I worked at a newspaper. The photo editor welded our staff into something amazing. At one time, we were a team of 14 and would have social gatherings where it was not unusual for all 14 to be there with their partners. There was a real feeling of family in the department.

The photo editor was autocratic in some ways, but he had a way of talking with people, of being involved with them and making them feel a part of the team. We all felt part of the team and reflected in the department's glory. The news photography that came out of our department would have been equal to or better than any in the world. This was the first time I noticed a team was more than the sum of the individuals—I didn't know the word then but there was synergy present.

So you are now able to identify some of the elements that distinguish synergy?
Yes. A key factor is that everybody feels he or she has something valuable to contribute. And the less autocratic a leader is, the more people feel a part of what's happening and the more synergy is present. Where decisions rise out of a group rather than being imposed on it, they work better.

In the photo department then, there was room for people to show their full potential?
Yes. The best times were when we felt we were in training. We hired a younger photographer who was always inquiring. He always wanted to do better and he reinforced us all in trying to do better—it wasn't competition, although that was present. We would look at the photographs and be constructively critical of them. We would talk about how they could have been taken better, so the photographers were always looking for ways to take better pictures.

Whenever I've been part of a group that considers itself in training—in other words we don't know everything—that's when extraordinary things happen.

So maybe being in training and coming from "not knowing" provides a space for synergy to show up?
Yes—not knowing and not knowing what's going to come out of something seem to increase your motivation. We rarely go along flat in life—we're either improving or getting worse. When we opt for aliveness—for being continually in training—synergy shows up.

There seems to be an element of a common purpose or shared vision in what you were up to?
Yes. Our purpose was simple. It was to get the best pictures into the paper so as to have the most impact. And our photographers won a lot of prizes in competitions. That wasn't the reason we did it, but it was great icing on the cake.

Excellence was showing up and it was being recognized by others?
Yes. Acknowledgment is important. The common purpose was important and, also, everybody felt appreciated. Both of the men I've mentioned always gave appreciation—I felt appreciated and I noticed many others did too. These men acknowledged people. And that's what I do in my own life. I think I always did tell people I appreciated them, but the contact with those men reinforced it in me. I know that whenever I do it, I get joy out of it.

I suppose what I do is facilitate the people I come into contact with. I do it by acknowledging them, but I get something out of it—it's not altruistic. I notice that when I'm appreciating and acknowledging people, I'm energized. It's not that I try to do it—it's just that when I notice I'm more alive, I realize I've been appreciating people. It probably became more obvious to me through my personal growth and counselor training.

What I was taught to do was to really listen to people, to listen to everything—their problems, hopes, fears, and dreams. I noticed that if you focused on the positive and gave space to the negative, people had room to change.

I ignored their "I can't do that," and concentrated and reinforced their positive side. It's a bit simplistic to say accentuate the positive and eliminate the negative—but that's the idea. The danger with eliminating the negative is you concentrate on it. Accentuate the positive and "give space" to the negative—don't ignore it, but don't take a lot of notice of it.

So what excites you is other people being excited? That's a self-expression for you?
Yes. I feel most alive when I'm enthusiastic—when I'm in the full flush of something that grabs me, and when I see my enthusiasm has enthused someone else—it's like a drug. I love inspiring others and I love being inspired. When I was about 15 a friend was a real enthusiast for Italian opera and he got me totally enthusiastic about it. In college he was inspired by D. H. Lawrence, Thomas Mann and Herman Hesse and he inspired me to read them and I've now read most of their books. I became passionate about them and still find them a joy to read. That was my friend inspiring me. In turn, I've inspired others in similar ways.

I've heard you describe yourself as a life enthusiast and that's really what you're talking about now?
Yes. What I love doing is turning somebody else on to something that turns me on. That's just a joy. It's like a recognition. Say you're at a party and you talk about a book and you say, "I loved it," and the other person enthusiastically says, "So did I"—you feel a recognition between you.

So part of enthusiasm for you is recognition—getting to the heart of the matter?
We are all alone in the world, but the moments that make us feel connected and human are when we "recognize" something that someone's done and we say "Yes," and realize that in that area of life we are not alone. Perhaps the more experiences you have like that, the more whole you are as a human.

There's a phrase I've always liked about always looking for "the pattern which connects" and that seems to be a very similar concept to recognizing yourself. The idea goes wider than humanity; it goes for the whole of life and inanimate things like the planets, the moon and the tides. I've noticed that rituals are more powerful when you tie them in with an outside pattern—like the moon. If we connect with existing patterns, the rituals are more powerful.

So it's a whole cosmic element. There are connections between individuals and individuals connect with the tides and the moon and the elements. The pattern which connects is like a universal—like the micro and the macro?
Yes—as above, so below, as the astrologers say. In the subatomic world, it's been found that when a scientist looks hard enough for an undiscovered particle, he'll probably find it. It's almost as if he invented it. That seems remarkably similar to: "We create our own reality."

It's interesting to look in these terms at what can happen with groups of people. How would you relate groups to the possibility of creating your own reality?
With a group, somehow, you can be more than you are as an individual. I've noticed that in the way we three as authors operate. When I'm with Dale and Anne, and we've dealt with our baggage, I'm more than I am as an individual. It's partly that they expect me to be more—the positive elements of me are amplified and the negative parts are ignored.

As an individual, that's quite hard to do. As an individual, it's hard for me to ignore a sore toe. But if I'm in a group of people who are inspiring me and who I am inspiring, and they won't listen to me complain about my sore toe, then I forget about it and concentrate on other things. I become more than I can be alone.

It's not that I don't deal with the sore toe, but the group enables me to look more at the possibilities and be less concerned with the negatives. That's what's available in groups.

The *possibility of us* is enhanced by being in a group.

It's always empowering when I have to extend myself a little more in the drumming group I play with. When we get together as drummers, we become better drummers than we are as individuals. When I'm with others I drum better. It's synergistic.

If groups—family, workplace, communities—operate in this way, what would flow out of that?
The sky is the limit. I don't think there is anything that groups can't achieve. One of the keys I while identified working on the last book was the idea that facilitating a group or a person is about knowing that the group or person has the answer. You haven't got the answer as facilitator, they have. And if you start giving them the answer, it's not facilitation and it doesn't work.

In my family, my being a father hasn't worked when I try to tell my children what to do. When I give them advice and tell them how to do things, it doesn't work. If I have faith that they know the answer and suspend my judgment and maybe help them find the answer, our relationship is enhanced. Honoring someone and dropping the judgment is the most difficult and important thing.

Is it important for a facilitator to master dropping judgments or find a way to set them aside?
It's vital. Maybe a facilitator can make the judgment and then set it aside—and by recognizing it as a judgment not take it into account. When I recognize and own my own prejudices, to some extent it frees me from them. In journalism, I've found that bias happens when writers don't recognize their prejudices.

You can't really drop a judgment until you recognize it?
That's true—we need to recognize it first.

Can you talk a little about some of the key skills and attributes that you think a facilitator needs to have?
The first attribute is an ongoing self-awareness. A facilitator needs to be in training all the time. That's the key. As a facilitator,

I am always looking at myself, always aware of my prejudices as much as I can be. Without that I can't even start facilitating. You've got to work on yourself first. Without awareness of your own triggers, your own baggage, you are going to get tripped up all the time with other people's baggage and not realize it.

What kinds of training have you found particularly useful?
The best self-awareness training is the training that turns you on. A young man once asked Joseph Campbell what he needed to do. Campbell said: "Follow your bliss." That's how you succeed in life. Find out what turns you on and do it. In terms of training, anything that helps you look at yourself is worthwhile. And there's such a wide range of training available. The ones that have been most valuable to me are the ones I was really excited about at the time.

When I look back, the first area of training that was helpful to me was encounter groups—they were really exciting and they impinged on the area of sexuality, which has always been a leading edge for me.

The other very important one for me was the co-counseling training I did 14 years ago with Dale and Anne. Apart from the fact that that was where I met Dale and Anne, I *recognized* myself in co-counseling. I'm not a practicing co-counselor now in the sense that I actually have sessions, but I live that way. I believe every person has his or her own right answers. I treat others as perfect the way they are—that ties in very strongly for me with the whole concept of this book.

So the best training is the training that turns you on, that you get excited about, and that can be anything. Anything at all?
Yes, anything.

John Heron

What does group facilitation mean to you?
To me, it means empowering people to be self-determining in the context of a relationship with other self-determining people. So it's about the interaction between autonomy and cooperation in human beings, and enabling people to develop this, enjoy it and affirm more of it in their lives.

What are the values behind your approach to facilitation?
The fundamental values in my approach to facilitation are intrinsically worthwhile human states. One of these is autonomy, where people are empowered in freedom to realize and fulfill their own true needs and interests. That realization is only possible in relation with other persons who are similarly engaged.

As I said at the outset, I can only be a self-determining person in relation with other self-determining persons. So another primary value is that of cooperation: creative interaction, interdependence, corporate endeavor between people.

A third value, which in the early days of the facilitation business was underappreciated, was what I call *hierarchy*. This means deciding for others and thinking for others, and exercising liberating power over others. This is a value when it's not distorted into its oppressive, improper forms.

Could you give an example of that?
There is a deep sense in which people, particularly in this sort of society and this culture, need leading into freedom. It's the paradox of the charismatic leader wisely deciding things for others, in order to release in those people their own autonomy and cooperation.

For example, when I'm running a basic co-counseling training, I don't ask the participants to help plan the course. I indicate what's involved and seek broad assent to the program, but basically I decide for the group the different stages of the training. Only when people are well into it would we get into the consultative mode. In a follow-up or advanced workshop, it would be entirely in the consultative, cooperative mode in which I say: "Let's put together what you're interested in and what I have to offer and see what kind of a creative contract we can make."

In training facilitators, I teach that the competent trainer is one who can move flexibly between the three forms of power in the positive sense:

❏ Power over—deciding for.
❏ Power with or power shared with—deciding cooperatively with people and negotiating.
❏ Delegating power to—handing over the decisions to people to make autonomously.

What's empowering about facilitation is the ability to move appropriately between these three decision modes. Hierarchy, deciding for others for a period, is only legitimate if the ultimate goal is the liberation of cooperation and autonomy. As these start to emerge, there's a shift and the facilitator slips over into the correlative modes of cooperative decision-making and delegated decision-making.

Many facilitators shy away from authority because old paradigm authority has been distressed and oppressive, rather than liberating. They often need a little encouragement to exercise new paradigm, distress-free authority and assume appropriately the fullness of their authentic personal power. In training facilitators, I always include charismatic training.

You say charismatic training—in what way?

Each person has idiosyncratic personal power and presence, and there's a huge taboo in the culture which gives a message to all children: "Don't be joyful, don't be autonomous, and above all, don't be the extraordinarily radiant, charismatic, spiritual being you essentially are."

Some facilitators-in-training have a tendency to make the chest concave so the heart goes back, to negate the whole of the lower body, to stick out the jaw and talk too much. In the training, I rearrange the posture and say: "Let's start with being present. Be aware of your whole physical gesture in space." If a facilitator feels the fullness of his or her bearing in this way, it starts to magnetize the group. It brings about a subtle shift of energy.

Then the facilitator can put an important *up-hierarchy* to work, in which what is above emerges out of, is shaped, supported and empowered by, what is below. So the feeling of presence shapes the tone and timing of the voice, which in turn shapes the choice of words, which influence the ideas, which affect the whole purpose of the interaction.

This up-hierarchy—from presence to tone and timing of the voice to choice of language to thought to the purpose of what the facilitator is about—is a very effective training tool. It enables the facilitator to become empowered from within, to find basic simplicity of being; and this is immediately communicated to the group. If he or she speaks in what I call *charismatic time,* the whole group will go into a light trance, in which members' aspirations, energies and potentials rise up toward realization.

When a group is in that sort of trance, I overtly and specifically affirm all kinds of suggestions and sow all kinds of seeds. It's this aspect of facilitation which in the early days people tended to shy away from, wanting to rush in with consultative, participant-centered decision-making far too soon.

The ability to be self-empowering and to assume charismatic presence and command in order to initiate everybody into their own internal space where they can empower themselves is an important part of the business. That's what I mean by valid, distress-free authority in a facilitator. It is often a fruitful precursor to the emergence of autonomy and cooperation in the group. When these emerge, the facilitator's decision mode switches over into consultation and delegation.

Could you talk about the transpersonal side of facilitation?
Facilitation is a form of authentic theater where I play myself and encourage everybody else to play themselves. To play oneself is an interesting paradox—there is no pretense or simulation. If you play yourself, you don't pretend anything precisely because it is yourself you are playing. It's original drama. You portray who you really are. And you do this by using the up-hierarchy. You empower yourself by becoming present and allowing tone, timing, language, thought and purpose to emerge out of that. This is a transpersonal process—you are allowing some immanent power within to shape your unique expression. You let your distinctive behavior well up out of some presence far more deeply interfused. What you say and do is a personal manifestation of some movement of the spirit within.

There's an inner source, a wellspring of personal potential and it's an accessible mystery. All you have to do is stand up and feel the whole of your gesture in space, feel your presence within the world, and you're open to this wellspring.

I believe there is a deep connection between consciousness and space.

The idea that mind and space are totally separate and that mind has none of the properties of space and space has none of the properties of mind is an out-of-date Cartesian model. Space is a form of consciousness, not just my consciousness, but universal consciousness. My consciousness is a local eddy in the space of a universal one. All I have to do to open to the universal one is to feel with full awareness my spatial presence and I'm there.

Once you enter this local experiential space, you realize it is not constrained by the boundaries of the physical body, and you can open out to a vast experiential space within and beyond it. All our experiential spatial fields interpenetrate within this vast inner space. These interweaving spatial fields are also energy fields so that to open awareness to them is to live with enhanced energy.

Culture conditions us to see each other as physical objects in terms of physical perspectives. Then I identify too much with an external view of you as a physical form in my perceptual field. But if I feel my presence and extend it to interpenetrate with your felt presence—your *feel* of your being in space—those two experiential fields interpenetrate. If I cultivate this awareness, then I live in two interpenetrating worlds—one is the perspectival world of physical space and the other is the experiential world of shared inner space.

That is a fundamental aspect of group dynamics. I can move across the room and stand beside you as if I'm just doing something in physical or perspectival space or I can be aware that I'm actually walking in and through a shared experiential field. The whole thing is subtly different if I walk with this sort of awareness. It becomes a transpersonal process.

The shared experiential, *inter-mental* field, which we're all participating in, is relatively unconscious. At present it is a tacit part of reality because not many people are functioning in it with any kind of awareness. A facilitator needs to tune in to it. I would never facilitate without resonating with it, and what I then do emerges out of the whole shared field.

Some people who promote the transpersonal, such as Assagioli and his egg diagram, use the old patriarchal model of the divine as transcendent. That diagram has the transpersonal self right up at the very top and everybody says: "However do we get up there?" So people use active imagination to go up mountains to meet wise old men.

This overlooks the divine as immanent, immediately accessible through personal presence in the way that I have described. To pursue the transcendent only is to make spiritual practice apart from living, take it into time-out. To open to the immanent, through experiential space and experiential timing, is to live the life of expressive spirit.

The prefix *trans* in *transpersonal* is systematically ambiguous. It can mean *beyond* as in *transcendent;* or it can mean *through* as in *transparent;* or it can mean *changing from one state to another* as in *transform.* The latter two senses affirm divine immanence, the spirit shining through and transforming the person.

How would you relate all this to group consciousness? It seems that what's available out of that would be very powerful?
We come here to the *holonomic principle,* thought by radical physicists, systems theorists, and others to be fundamental in the scheme of things. This principle asserts that the whole is represented in the part—the whole hologram is represented in any part of the holographic plate; the whole of the tacit universe is represented in any part of the explicit universe. Poets have affirmed this: Blake's "universe in a grain of sand."

I think there are certainly occasions in which the whole group is represented by one of its members: one person in the group will raise an issue which is right on line for sorting out what the whole group wants to do; or what one person does is a surrogate for the doing of the total group. Facilitators need to be, at least some of the time, holonomic in the sense that what they are doing is a focus for the energy and dynamic, the needs and concerns, of the group as a whole. Tuning in to the shared experiential field is a way of enabling that to happen. That's what a facilitator does.

There's another very interesting way of working with the holonomic principle through ritual. I have used it many times. After I explain the holonomic principle, everyone writes his or her name on a piece of paper, which is put into a basket. Then each in turn picks a piece of paper out, reads the name and hands the basket to the person whose name is on the piece of paper. The last person whose name is picked out is the holonomic focus.

Once this person is selected, he or she goes ceremonially around the group, shakes each member by the base of the nose and says: "I empower you to learn and grow." The effect can be quite extraordinary, producing a total shift of consciousness in the whole group. The whole is more than the part and can be revealed through the part. The whole group can get in touch with its full power when that power is focused through one person and bestowed through that person to everyone in the group.

Another way is for the holonomic focus, also chosen by a ritual of the arbitrary, to be the *guru* and to sit on a throne. Everyone plays the theater in earnest. Anyone is moved goes up to the guru and asks whatever searching questions come to mind such as: "What is the meaning of life?" or "What's the meaning of my life?"

It is noticeable how the holonomic focus, ritually bequeathed to one person in the group, empowers that person to respond to the questions in a way that is truly luminous. People get deeper and deeper into the theater and that's just a way of proving the holonomic point. It is a remarkable process.

In one group everyone took his or her left sock off and put it into a sack to find the holonomic focus. The last sock to be picked out belonged to an elderly retired lawyer. I don't know how he'd gotten into the group. He was a nice man who had probably thought: "I'll try something new in my retirement instead of going to Russian classes." When he realized he was to be the focus he said: "I can't do this, I can't." I said: "It's the contract. You are the one. It's come your way, go with it."

So, being a conscientious person, he realized he had to do it and he sat on the throne. It was extraordinary, for suddenly the holonomic power took him over. He was a good man with a lifetime of experience relating to all kinds of crises and problems and all that welled up, transformed by the holonomic principle. He became a transfigured luminary. Group members were lining up to ask him questions. And when it was all over and he had been deroled, he just turned back into this diffident retired lawyer, the power gone. It was quite extraordinary.

You've been teaching facilitation in various countries for some time now. Have you noticed changes, movements? Is facilitation becoming more widespread?

It's become more widespread in the last few years in that people involved in staff-development units are expected to know something about facilitation. So in that sense it has become a very significant minority culture in the education and training world. It certainly wasn't in the '70s. It's the whole education revolution—the realization that learning is necessarily self-directed, that a lot of teaching does not guarantee a lot of learning. Learning requires interest, commitment, retention and understanding, all of which are self-generated. I can't do your learning for you; I can only facilitate the process in you.

The educational shift is from how to teach to how to facilitate learning. With the realization that learning is autonomous goes the idea that it needs to be holistic—that intellectual propositions need to be brought into relation with the learner's experience and action. To facilitate such autonomous and holistic learning requires emotional development and interpersonal skill on the part of the facilitator.

And this view, that the personal and professional development of the facilitator are interdependent, now has a significant foothold in many education and training establishments, among a spearhead minority. In terms of methodology, this creative minority is busy with the experiential learning cycle, with suggestive accelerated learning, with learning contracts, self- and peer assessment, collaborative assessment, and so on.

What about consensus decision-making—using facilitation, say, in a committee structure—to get a consensus decision?
A very important arm of facilitation is its direct political application in running meetings and in decision-making in organizations. The facilitator needs to be aware of the three decision modes: direction—deciding for others; negotiation—deciding with others; and delegation—handing over decision-making to others. The effective and empowering facilitator, as I said earlier, is one who can move flexibly, appropriately and openly between these three decision modes.

Somewhere between negotiation and delegation the facilitator simply acts as chairperson to enable the group to reach a decision. Such a chairperson needs be very clear about decision procedures: Is it a simple majority vote, three-quarters majority vote, unanimity, gathering the sense of the meeting or consensus? The facilitator needs to help the group choose a model, then stick to it; and only change it intentionally after a decision/procedure review.

*Majority decision-making is an us-and-them type model—that's
what democracy is. We believe we all need to move toward cooperative ways of thinking and discover models which reinforce
that so people can work together on an international scale.*
Yes. I like that a lot. The idea of going from crude majority vote
as in democracy to cooperacy, in which minorities are fully
honored and understood and cherished and then can agree to go
along with what the majority want, is a good one.

Another version is the Quaker one of gathering the sense of
the meeting. We discuss the issues and if someone feels they've
got the sense of it they'll say: "I feel the sense of the meeting is
this and what we're really saying is we want to do that." Then
people say: "No that's not it," and there's more discussion, until
eventually someone does gather the sense of the meeting. When
everyone says: "Yes, that's it," they know they've got it.

Do you see any limitations to facilitation?
There are moral limitations, and there's degenerate facilitation. It
degenerates when the facilitator gets stuck in counter-transfer-
ence and starts to punish the group for some unfinished business
in his or her own past, like trying to heal his or her dysfunctional
family of origin. If I'm endlessly trying to recreate in a group the
happy family I never had, and I'm not aware of it, that's a degeneration. But it's not as bad as unconsciously punishing the group
because it reminds me of the bad family I had.

There's a close analogy between group process and what John
Southgate calls the *creative orgasmic cycle*. If the facilitator isn't in
touch with the parallelism between sexuality and facilitation, it
can skew the facilitation subtly through unaware symbolic seduction, invasion or rejection. Then there's classic manipulation
where I get the group to do what satisfies my interests, regardless
of whether it satisfies the interests of the group. I think there are

various pathologies in degeneration and they blur over into obvious immoralities, like charging too much money and explicit sexual seduction, which of course have been rife through the helping professions, presumably since time immemorial.

In terms of its positive limits, facilitation is a creatively self-annihilating role. It's self-limiting if it's done well. A person who is empowering others to be interdependently autonomous and cooperative, which is very similar to cooperacy, is sooner or later going to be unneeded.

What about distress? Is there a need for people to have some way of getting get rid of distress? You obviously use co-counseling.
Yes. A balance needs to be found between two complementary ways of dealing with distress emotion. One is emotional discharge or catharsis, the process of releasing the distress; and the other is transmutation, changing the frequency of the emotional pain by consciousness-transforming methods.

Whichever method is used, I don't think a simple hydraulic model is relevant, like there's a big pool of distress inside you and if you pump it all out, or evaporate it all off, you'll be home free. That has been a popular theoretical model, but its a delusion and is itself a pathology. It denies something else, which is that order is permanently emerging out of chaos.

James Hillman's view is that souls continually pathologize their existence in order to grow. So the more you grow, the more you generate new bits of disorder and chaos because they are at the leading edge of further growth. As I develop, and because I develop, I become open to whole new dimensions of chaos I had been unaware of. And I feel vulnerable and it exposes raw parts of me and then I learn to cope with it. It seems sensible to suppose that that's a continuous process. It's very reassuring to creative souls—there's always abundant chaos around the corner.

So in terms of a group, it would be useful for it to build in some sort of way of accessing or bringing this to the surface?

Yes. A group needs to hang in with the mess and the chaos. Peter Reason and I have done a lot of work using the new research paradigm of cooperative inquiry, which is research *with* people, not *on* them. If you do research on people then you are directing them and it's not research on persons. If you're directing them, they're not being real persons, who are by definition self-directing.

The only way you can do research with real persons is if they are engaged as co-researchers in originating, managing and drawing conclusions from the data; and if they are also involved as co-subjects in the experience and action that is being researched. So everyone involved in the research moves between phases of reflection and of experience in a series of cycles of inquiry.

When you go into an experiential phase, if you're really open to it, the ideas you start with may evaporate and for a time both phases may become chaotic. Denis Postle, who wrote a book on catastrophe theory, was part of an early inquiry group. He noticed the chaos and said: "Look, I think we're rushing for premature closure. We're all extremely anxious so we are trying to tidy the mess up too soon." And immediately we thought: "My God, yes, we've got to hang in there."

We now hold it as a validity principle in cooperative inquiry that the group needs to tolerate chaos, be with it, live it, own it, not try to fight it off, and suffer it until order starts to emerge out of it. Premature pursuit of order is at the expense of the validity of that order—it'll be warped or evasive or too tidy. So I think tolerance of chaos is essential in a group.

What's your vision for the future?

I'm interested in creating and being part of a self-generating culture, that is, a group of people who live in the same neighborhood and create their own culture—rituals devised to give meaning to life and social practices to do with decision-making, economic subsistence, ownership, intimacy, education and all the rest of it. They create this and review it from time to time. It's like cooperative inquiry lived as a culture. Religion, too, will be experiential and inquiry-based, not dogmatic and authority-based.

My sense is that human culture is moving in two polar directions. One is toward increased decentralization—cooperation and autonomy exercised in relatively small neighborhoods in every aspect of life. There is commitment to sustainability, eco-synergy, permaculture and all those things—a human-scale, fully participative, sustainable lifestyle in a self-generating, self-renewing culture.

As that increases, what you'll need at the opposite pole are truly awe-inspiring structures of federalism. A unified planetary culture can't just consist of little neighborhoods. There also needs to be some form of corporate or federal interaction, which I don't think the "small is beautiful" people and the sustainable-neighborhood people have yet fully come to terms with.

Such federating structures presuppose new levels of information technology. And we shall delegate to the people in them wide-ranging hierarchical powers. We shall say: "Look, you can't be consulting us all the time, even by global referenda using high technology. You've got to make some decisions on our behalf."

So there'll be this remarkable polarity between autonomy and cooperation, highly developed in sustainable neighborhoods, and authorized hierarchy exercised at a global federal level. That seems to me to be a very interesting way that human culture may slowly unfold.

Does that tie in with the whole idea of facilitation?

I think facilitation as a concept needs to get out of the group room and into the world, which is a more vital place to be facilitative in than the group room. So in these neighborhoods facilitation will be essential.

Basically it's cooperation and autonomy, but in many situations someone will have to be a focal point and facilitate what's going on in these communities, using all three decision modes and that would lead to cooperacy.

We've thought a lot about the possibilities of synergy in terms of group synergy, with the whole being greater than the parts. What do you think is available out of that?
I think the whole is greater than the parts. There's a clear relation between the notion of synergy as you're using it and the notion of holonomy. Any dyadic relationship is creating something in which the togetherness—the *we*—can't be reduced back to the aggregate of the two *I*'s. So *we*, once we get going, is an entity in its own right, of which you and I are focal points. The reality is in the relationship between us. You and I as distinct beings are the epicenters, but the reality is in the field that includes us.

We've been thinking about whether group consciousness is the next big leap in human consciousness. There's been so much work done in personal development and individuality, but perhaps the next thing is group consciousness? The possibility of it is so enormous and amazing.
I agree. We are, whether we choose to notice it or not, participating in a shared inter-mental, experiential field which is the ground of our being present together in any group. This field in turn, I believe, interweaves with a dazzling array of other diverse fields within the experiential space of an all-inclusive consciousness.

And being conscious about that will give us a lot more power— there'll be so much more available. I absolutely agree.
Yes. It will totally transform the way we relate.

It's exciting, isn't it?
Yes it is.

Part 4

Resources

Contract Confirmation Model

Here is a model letter confirming a facilitation contract.

Sender's Address
Date
Name
Job Title
Organization
Address

Dear
This is to confirm my facilitation of the . . . (process) with . . .
(group).

The purpose of the process is to . . .

A planning meeting was held . . . (where and when) with . . .
(names of people present).

We agreed on the following outcomes:
(Make sure they are SMART—see pages 136-137.)

   1.
   2.
   3.

Outcomes will be measured by

    1.

    2.

    3.

(Be specific about who will do the measuring and by when.)

The agreed/proposed process is attached.

The cost of this service is $ . . . to be paid (terms—for example, within 14 days of the workshop). Please note that there is a cancellation fee of $ . . . if the workshop is canceled with less than . . . notice.

If you wish to discuss any of the above matters further please contact me (phone and/or fax) by . . . (date).

Yours sincerely,

(signature)

(typed name)

Meeting Record Sheet Model

This is a suggested meeting record sheet for all types of meetings
Adapt it for each specific purpose.

Meeting Record

Date and Time:
Meeting:
Purpose:
People attending:
Facilitator:
Venue:

Agenda items

    1.
    2.
    3.
    4.
    5.

Agenda item no.	Decision	Person responsible	Completion date	Status*

*completed, deleted or carried forward

Reading List

Self-facilitation

Creative Visualization. Shakti Gawain. Mill Valley Publishing. 1978.
Living in the Light. Shakti Gawain. Mill Valley Publishing. 1986.
The Power is Within You. Louise L. Hay. Specialist Publications. 1991.
The Seven Habits of Highly Effective People. Stephen R. Covey. The Business Library. 1990.
You Can Heal Your Life. Louise L. Hay. Hay House. 1987.

Facilitating Others

Getting The Love You Want. Harville Hendricks. Schwartz & Wilkinson. 1988.
Helping the Client. John Heron. Sage Publications. 1990.
Loving Relationships. Sondra Ray. Celestial Arts. 1980.
Loving Relationships II. Sondra Ray. Celestial Arts. 1992.

General

Confessions of a Janus Brain. John Heron. Endymion Press. 1987.
The Facilitators' Handbook. John Heron. Kogan Page. 1989.
Feeling and Personhood. John Heron. Sage Publications. 1992.
In the Tiger's Mouth: An Empowerment for Social Action. Katrina Shields. Millenium Books. 1991.
Power from Within: A Feminist Guide to Ritual Making. Juliet Batten. Istar Books. 1988.
Truth or Dare. Starhawk. Harper and Row. 1987.
Women Who Run with the Wolves. Clarissa Pinkola Estes. Rider Books. 1993
The Zen of Groups—A Handbook for People Meeting with a Purpose. Dale Hunter, Anne Bailey and Bill Taylor. Fisher Books. 1995.

Index

Bold text indicates major or defining references.
Italic text indicates processes from the Toolkit.